Adventures in Marine Collecting

ADVENTURES IN MARINE COLLECTING

Robert P. L. Straughan

South Brunswick and New York:
A. S. Barnes and Company
London: Thomas Yoseloff Ltd

A. S. Barnes and Co., Inc.
Cranbury, New Jersey 08512

Thomas Yoseloff Ltd
108 New Bond Street
London W1Y OQX, England

ISBN 0-498-01368-5
Printed in the United States of America

TO ROSEMARY, PAUL, AND JULIE

Contents

Preface

Skin divers are invading the quiet domain of the sea in ever increasing numbers. For hundreds of years, man has sailed blindly across the seas with scarcely a thought about the wondrous world beneath his ship. Swimmers by the millions seldom got more than a blurry glimpse of Neptune's wonderland.

But now, with the simple face mask, man can look into this strange, new world and see it as clearly and vividly as the world above. Once a swimmer has peered through a mask at the mystic land beneath the sea, he will never again want to swim blindly over the surface, for now he can swim with purpose. He can dive and explore, shoot a fish for dinner, or catch a colorful fish for his aquarium. He can look for pirate gold or take pictures of the new world he has discovered, and he can become an explorer anywhere the water beckons. With all this to offer, skin diving is destined to become the world's greatest sport to be enjoyed by young and old.

R. S.

Acknowledgments

To Thomas Yoseloff, who published my first comprehensive book on Salt Water Aquariums, and whose faith in skin diving and fish catching as a hobby encouraged me to complete this book. I am also indebted to Mr. F. G. Wood, Jr., of Marine Studios, Florida, who has helped me many times to be more scientifically accurate in my writings. Also, I am very thankful to Marine Studios for the use of their splendid photos which appear in the book, and to Paul Zahl who encouraged me to record my first-hand diving experiences. I am also indebted to Dr. F. G. Walton Smith of the Marine Laboratory, who realized my ambitions to become a collector and who dissuaded me from becoming an ichthyologist.

Introduction

Bringing them back alive is the most challenging and rewarding aspect of skin diving. It is not difficult to shoot a fish with a speargun or catch it on a hook and line, but it requires considerable adroitness to catch a fish alive in a small handnet in the labyrinth of a coral reef. It adds purpose to a dive when a skin diver can combine his hobby with a catch for his home aquarium. The thrill of outwitting and capturing a colorful marine beauty is unparalleled in any other sport.

A marine collector's job is one of the most fascinating and interesting professions that exists in the world today. Every trip is a new adventure and the collector becomes a true explorer, for his workshop is the fantastic fairyland of the coral reef. The beauty of a calm sea, a spectacular undersea garden, sunken Spanish Galleons, and the myriad of exotic tropical fish are commonplace to the collector, but never cease to amaze. Life under the sea, however, is not always serene: man-eating sharks, giant green moray eels, vicious barracuda, and other predators of the sea are ever present and may suddenly make an appearance when least expected.

The diver who spends any time underwater must learn to expect an encounter with any one of these monsters of the deep, whether he is close to shore, in waist deep water, or out on the deep reefs. Fierce tropical storms, poisonous jellyfish, stinging coral, and long spined sea urchins, add still another touch of danger to the life of the collector, but in our hectic world with its traffic jams, smoky cities, and crowded beaches, these dangers seem but a small price to the skin diving collector when he heads out to sea in his boat on a quiet tropical night, under a star studded sky.

Adventures
in Marine
Collecting

My Workshop Is the Sea

No factory bells or office walls
No climbing stairs to endless halls
No noisy streets and endless chatter
Nor smoky fumes, my lungs to shatter.

Instead I breathe the morning mist
I feel the bow, with gentle list
I see the world I've grown to love
My road map is the stars above.

My work clothes are my mask and fins
My tools are nets. My courage thins.
It's lonely as a man can be
My workshop is the silent sea.

R.P.L.S.

The author with his first successful diving helmet made from a galvanized hot water tank. It had both an air check valve and a bleeder valve. For a homemade helmet it was very efficient and was used to explore the quiet depths of New England lakes and ponds. (Photo courtesy Charles Svenson)

1
The First Dive

MY INTEREST IN THE SEA STEMS FROM EARLIEST CHILDHOOD when at the age of three my parents first brought me to the seashore off the New England coast. I immediately started "beachcombing" and, with youthful energy, began collecting what appeared to be dozens of dead crabs, dropping them excitedly into a large paper bag. The seashore seemed literally covered with the interesting creatures and my mother could hardly restrain herself with laughter for I had failed to notice that the very first crab I collected had soaked a large hole in the bottom of the bag and I was picking up the same one or two crabs over and over again!

This first initial encounter with the sea evidently moulded its everlasting impression in my mind, for although my youthful ambitions varied from being a wild animal trainer to an explorer, they invariably came back to the sea. I had my first diving experience at the age of twelve when a friend, Warren Prince, and myself engineered our first diving helmet. It consisted of a large metal wastepaper basket with a glass window in the front. The air hose was a section of garden hose, and the pump was a small hand bellows borrowed from the fireplace in Warren's home. Baptist pond, in Chelmsford, Mass., was the sight selected for the dive, and a deep spot close to shore was chosen. I donned the helmet and amid cheers of a small local audience, I stepped off into the deep water while my friend pumped the bellows. Everything went fine except that after the splash had died down, I found that I was not underwater. The air in the "helmet" acted as a float and kept me nearly a foot out of the water. I was hauled back to shore and it was quickly decided that I needed weight to hold me down. Nearby was a pile of granite blocks weighing about twenty pounds each and several of these were tied securely about my waist. Then, after several minutes of signal instructions, I descended once more into the water. This time I went straight down and soon hit the bottom. I was amazed! Fish were swimming about and I was in a strange underwater world. The steady throb of the air pump resounded in my ears and I felt like a true explorer on my first real adventure. I was down for several minutes when trouble started. Water began seeping into the helmet at an alarming rate and soon my vision became a blurr as the water rose over my head. I signalled frantically on the hand lines but no one pulled me up until finally in desperation I started climbing out by myself. This prompted quick action from shore and I was soon hauled to safety. Everyone expected me to be alright but their expressions turned to horror when they saw that the helmet was filled with water and I was desperately holding my breath. A small fish had somehow managed to get inside the helmet and was swimming around my face when the contraption was finally removed. The trouble was soon located, and it was discovered that the putty used to hold the glass in place was not waterproof. The glass had started to come loose and was allowing water to enter the helmet. On the surface, since plenty of bubbles were coming up, my friends had assumed that I was getting sufficient air, but down below it was another story.

My next diving helmet, built after I'd completed a tour of duty with the U.S. Navy, was much more successful and was put together with considerable effort by my oldest brother Jesse and myself. The base for this improved model was a galvanized hot water tank. Jesse cut out the proper shape with his acetylene torch, and with the aid of his welding outfit we made a good, workable helmet. I placed a double check-valve in the helmet so that air would not escape, and the window was made of quarter-inch plexiglass, which my friend Warren's father had donated for the cause. We needed a dependable air pump, and since we could find none for sale, we decided to build one. We had a vague idea of how they worked, so again Jesse and I shopped around for suitable machinery. We finally bought a length of four-inch boiler pipe and made a very efficient double-action air pump. Altogether with extension handles the pump was eight feet long and nearly three feet high. It took two men to carry it and it was painted bright red. It was an impressive piece of equipment and furnished more than enough air.

This time, the expedition was carried out in a small stream in Pelham, N.H., and my good friend Charlie Svenson and I were the official divers. Lead shoes were used so that we would stay right side up, and a rather sizeable crowd gathered to watch the event. I dove first and Charlie manned the pump. Everything went perfectly, and soon I was walking on the bottom of the creek. Charlie was pumping air with the giant pump and huge bubbles broke the surface. This seemed to fascinate him and he pumped all the harder. He soon found that by pumping fast he could lift me right off the bottom and this appealed to his great sense of humor, for as soon as he thought I was settled on the bottom, he would give a series of rapid pumps and send me bouncing out of the water. The homemade helmet and pump functioned perfectly and Charlie and I spent a great deal of time exploring the local ponds and lakes. We made underwater "sifters" and would visit swimming areas where there were high diving boards and deep water. We would work in a depth of forty feet or more, sifting the sand on the bottom for "treasure." We found all sorts of things, including numerous coins, rings, false teeth and bracelets. This was my first dive for treasure and it really paid off. We went from one lake to another, usually early in the morning and I eventually accumulated the largest collection of false teeth in town. Of course it was impossible to find their owners and eventually I melted the teeth down and made a huge gold nugget. I think I gave it to my brother Joe. We dove right up to the cold weather and I regretfully put away the gear for the following year. It had been an exciting summer.

I grew up with the sea in my blood and spent much of my time at the seashore. One summer I spent the entire summer vacation at Boothbay Harbor, Maine, with my good friend Sid Speed. We camped right by the sea in a large tent at Owl's Head and spent all our free time exploring the rocky shores. We went out with lobstermen, helping them pull their traps and marveling at the dogfish and other strange creatures they would bring up. We ate lobster for breakfast, lunch and dinner, even having them in our sandwiches as well as in soups and chowders. Each day was an adventure. We would row a skiff to offshore islands and explore. Many were rarely visited in those days and one in particular was "forbidden." It was said that anyone who was caught on the island would be shot! This was all we needed to hear to make us want to visit the island. We decided to go there early in the morning before sunrise so that no one would see us. It was an exciting plan.

We wasted no time and the next morning we were approaching the island in a skiff, which we had rowed over from the mainland. We rowed so quietly that we scarcely made a ripple in the water. We had practiced silent rowing and it paid off, for soon we were at the mysterious island. It was still dark as the boat gently nudged the shore and we waited quietly in the boat for the first light of dawn so we could see what we were doing. Then we silently walked ashore. It was a beautiful island, a pristine wilderness, with deep green moss blanketing the ground like a thick rug beneath the trees. We wondered why anyone would want to shoot someone if they came there. We walked on through the woods and then came to a clearing. At the edge there were deep tire tracks, apparently from a large truck. Then we heard voices, quite loud and close by. It was rapidly getting light and we decided to leave as quickly as possible. We hurried back to the boat and quickly pushed off from shore. When we were about a mile away we heard shots, but didn't know whether they were aimed at us or not. We bent the oars and rushed back to the mainland for a hearty breakfast of fresh-dug clams scrambled with eggs. It was like eating rubber bands but we were ravenously hungry after our early morning adventure. We didn't have enough eggs for a meal so I had decided to put in the clams to stretch the food. It was not too successful.

We didn't tell anyone we had been to the island for fear that someone might come looking for us, and spent the rest of the day wading the shallows probing for large rays, sea urchins and other forms of marine life. Sid and I had always fancied ourselves as adventurers. We grew up together in Chelmsford, Massachusetts, and had studied morse code, signaling, secret codes and survival in the wilds to prepare us for adventure. Now we were having adventure at its best. Then the war came.

Sid's father was a captain in the navy and commanded his own boat. I learned later, while I was overseas, that his father's ship had landed on one of the remote islands somewhere up in that area and had captured a fleet of German submarines, which had been using the island as a base right on our very shores. I've often wondered if it was the same island we had visited.

During the war, I served over three years with the U.S. Navy as a photographer and visited many interesting places in the Pacific, including Hawaii, Japan, China, the Philippines, the Mariannas, the Marshall Islands, and Okinawa. I spent much of my free time ashore collecting sea shells, finding the shell fish when they were still alive so that the shells would have the maximum in beauty and lustre. I dove along the reefs of many atolls often by myself and swam in the heavily shark infested waters in search of prize specimens. The best shells were collected from deep holes in the reef. I would dive to the bottom and reach my arm as far into the hole as I could. Then I would feel around inside for the smooth surface of the shells. I collected many rare beauties and often when I retracted my hands from the dark crevices, I would have a dozen or more long black needles hanging from my fingers. These were from the long-spined sea urchins, and although they were very painful, the effects seldom lasted longer than a few minutes. I often realize now how fortunate I was in those days not to have gotten bitten by a moray eel, or have put my bare hands on the deadly spines of a stone fish, known to inhabit the area. The stone fish is one of the deadliest creatures in the world, and a puncture from one of its spines is nearly always followed by agonizing death.

But luck was with me, for I went through the entire service without any serious mishaps.

After the war, I returned to the States and worked at various jobs in New England during the summer and as cold weather approached, I headed south like the birds. I had become very fond of diving and found that I could make a living in Florida where it was always warm, diving and exploring in my spare time. I still hadn't made up my mind what my life's work would be. I left the Navy as a Photographer's Mate First Class and had had considerable selling experience so that work was always easy for me to obtain, but I was still unsure about choosing something permanent. I wanted to work with the sea, but wasn't sure how to go about it. For years I had thought of building a huge aquarium to exhibit the strange and interesting creatures of the sea. In fact, my sole reason for going to Florida in the first place was to visit the world's first oceanarium at Marine Studios near St. Augustine, Florida. This was in 1942 and the war had just started. Marineland was closed, so I continued on down to Miami. One day I noticed a sketch of a proposed aquarium in the Miami paper by Walton Smith of the University of Miami, so I made an appointment to talk to him about the project. I had also heard about the marine biology course at the University and, since this seemed like an interesting field, I thought I would like to enroll in it. Dr. Smith interviewed me and elaborated on his proposed aquarium. I told of my interest in the Marine Biology Department and he enlightened me as to its true aspects. It was not as glamorous as I had envisioned, for it entailed much miscroscopic work, calculus, mathematics, and statistics. What appealed to me most was collecting the interesting creatures of the sea, not studying their bones through the microscope. I left the University still undecided about what I would do.

Then I decided I would become a deep-sea diver. I had heard about a diving school in California and wrote to them for particulars. They wrote back that first I must have a thorough physical examination to see if I was physically qualified for the rigors of deep-sea diving. I had the physical and sent the necessary forms back to the school and was told that I would be accepted for entry. Before heading to California, I decided to visit New England for a while to see my folks and my friends. There I met a former deep sea diver, Ed Marchand, who was a close friend of my aunt's and told him of my plan to enter diving school. He was not very impressed and spent many hours telling me of the actual work that divers must do to make a year-round living wage. Other than an occasional job by the police to locate a drowned person, there was little to be offered in the way of work for a professional diver, he advised me. Salvage companies or bridge builders need divers for certain parts of their work, but the work is often in out-of-the-way places and in extremely dirty water so that you would seldom see any fish life. Ed gave me a true picture of this often publicised "glamorous" work and I was deeply thankful to him for it.

I decided that at least for the time being, I wouldn't become a deep-sea diver, so instead of going to California I stayed in New England and opened a pet shop. I had as many as forty dogs on hand at a time and it was a howling success and fun besides. I went in for the unusual pet such as horned toads, lizards, wild crows, etc., and had a large display of tropical fish. During the warm summer weather, my old friend Charlie Svenson and myself would go to the ocean to collect small crabs, blennies, stickbacks, and other marine specimens and these were placed on exhibit in my first salt-water aquarium. Little did I realize at the time that one day collecting these interesting salt-water fish and specimens would be a full-time profession. I opened up a second pet shop in the downtown area but was still undecided as to what I would do for my life's work. I decided I did not want to run a pet shop for the rest of my life, so I sold out the merchandise and went to college at the University of New Hampshire.

This lasted about five months when I decided college life wasn't for me. I left the beautiful school and returned home for a few weeks still undecided about what to do. Winter was well on its way and I had developed a strong dislike for cold weather so I went to Arizona. I had always wanted to see the giant Suarara cactus trees there, and accomplished this by staying in this beautiful state for several months. I did a little prospecting for gold while I was there, too.

After Arizona, I landed in Dallas, Texas, where I got a job as a photo lithographer, at Ryan Litho Service, where I worked for a little over a year. It was a fine job and Bill Ryan, the owner, was a very nice man to work for, but I longed for the sea and wanted to get into underwater photography as I thought this might be a good way to make a living. One day, I regretfully told Bill that I was going to leave as I wanted to go back to Florida. He understood and wished me luck and after another trip to New England, I finally landed back in Florida where I am today. I had made one important change in Texas which I hadn't planned on. I got married to a Dallas girl named Rosemary. If Rose had known at the time, what a hectic, unstable, and worrisome career I would eventually choose for myself, she would probably have run away in the opposite direction rather than walk down the aisle with me on that memorable day.

2
I Become a Collector

ONCE BACK IN FLORIDA, I CONCENTRATED ALL MY EFFORTS
into forming a career that would lead to undersea work,
but it was a difficult task. I wanted most of all to become a
fish collector and capture live specimens for aquariums,
but had no idea how to get into the field. I had contacted
veteran marine collector Capt. William Grey in Miami
hoping that he could possibly give me a job, but at that
time he was working by himself and he said there just
wasn't enough work for two people. I told him of my intense interest in the sea and asked if I could go out on a
collecting trip with him. He was quite reluctant at first,
but finally consented to take me on a trip. I was thrilled
beyond words for I had a tremendous desire to see and
learn everything I possibly could about the coral reefs.
They had almost become a part of my life. I had written to
Capt. Grey from New England and he remembered my
letter. He said we would leave very early, even before
dawn so that we could get out to sea before the weather got
too rough and asked me to call him in the morning to see
if he was going out. The weather would be the deciding
factor for if it was too windy, we would have to wait for a
calm day.

It took about five days before the weather was right for a trip, but finally a calm day arrived. I was so anxious to go that I was down at the docks nearly an hour early. I knew it would be an interesting trip and Captain Grey had told me that if the weather held, we would stay out overnight and make it a two-day excursion. Captain Grey soon arrived and we headed out to sea. It was a long trip out to the reefs from the Miami docks, but the time passed swiftly. Capt. Grey knew so much about life in the sea that I was very much impressed. He had been near the sea nearly all his life and knew the ways and habits of all the sea creatures. I marveled at his strength as he pulled in huge fish traps several feet across, and when he told me that he usually went out all by himself, I felt it was very dangerous work for a man to do all alone. Little did I realize that some day I would be doing the very same thing, and, even more harrowing, I would be *diving* by myself.

The weather was good so we anchored in the protection of an island and spent the night. The first day we pulled traps and collected an interesting assortment of colorful fish in the huge live wells. The second day we dragged for sea horses in the bay and found all sorts of interesting specimens. I was so enthralled with collecting that I hated to go back home. This was exactly the kind of work I wanted to do. My trip with Captain Grey had settled my mind for good. Now I would have to find a way to do it.

Jobs were not too plentiful in Miami at the time, but I secured a job at Burdines department store selling cameras and photographic equipment. My days off and evenings were spent on the reefs or out in the Bay even when it was cold or raining. There would be times when I was the only person in the water in the entire area. I would dive until I turned blue with cold. I just couldn't get enough. I began to catch colorful little fish with a crude hand net and soon set up a salt-water aquarium in my home. I would skin dive both in the bay and in the Keys and I began to catch a wide assortment of creatures, which included large sea horses, cowfish, boxfish, pipefish, butterflyfish, and angel-fish. At first I took only enough for my own aquarium, but eventually began to collect extra specimens for a few of the local pet shops. At this stage, my collecting was purely a hobby, but it was the most enjoyable one I had ever known. I longed constantly to be able to do it as a full-time profession, but it was not possible at the time.

One day, one of my pet sea horses had several hundred babies and I became so fascinated watching them in the aquarium that I decided to make a movie of them. I took a hundred-foot roll of the father sea horse with his tremendous brood and, to my delight, it turned out surprisingly well, especially the extreme close-up shots of the large horse's strange head and snout. That single roll of film eventually played a major role in my future, for a short time later I met an old friend and former navy photographer, Ralph Bowden, who had stopped by the store to purchase some film. He was very surprised to see me and I was happy to see him as I had always regarded him as a close friend even though we had lost contact with each other through the years. Ralph was working in the Bahamas as a private photographer for a millionaire, and he invited me over to his home to see some of his movies. I stared in disbelief at the fantastic clearness of the water and the beautiful white sandy beaches. It looked like a paradise, and the way Ralph talked about it, I wished there was some way I could go there.

Ralph visited me a few more times on his brief trips back to Miami, always with breathless tales of the giant tuna, marlin, and sharks he had seen and photographed.

One time he brought over a Fen-Jon underwater movie camera and told me that he was going to start making underwater movies. The thought of it almost drove me mad because this is exactly what I wanted to do. I asked Ralph if he needed an assistant and he laughed and said he would see what he could do about it. Then I remembered my sea horse movie and I ran it off for him on my editing machine. He thought it was very interesting and wanted to borrow it to show to his boss.

Ralph's recent visits to my home had been more than just a friendly call, for one night he told me that he had been "feeling me out" about whether or not I would like to go to the Bahamas and help him with his photography. He finally told me that he had been promoted from photographer to manager and that the photograper job was open to me if I was interested. Was I! I couldn't wait to leave. Ralph had shown my sea horse movie to Mr. Lyon, his boss, who liked it, and had recommended me for the job on the basis of my Navy experience and my interest in the sea. In a short while Rosemary and I were on a sea plane headed for Bimini, British West Indies. It was a breath-taking sight as the plane settled down on the spectacular, emerald blue waters of the Bahamas. I had to pinch myself to be sure I wasn't dreaming.

We had a brand new apartment with everything furnished and I was to be the photographer while Rosemary would be a combination bookkeeper and radio operator. Ralph and I made several underwater movies, and I made many movies of leaping marlin, shooting the leaps with a high speed electric camera in slow motion. But the underwater movies were my greatest joy and I just couldn't get enough of them. Mr. Lyon and Ralph had given me freedom to photograph anything on the islands that would make an interesting movie, and when I wasn't on the boats photographing marlin, I could work on interesting projects ashore. I would photograph tiny curly tailed lizards, crabs, birds, and anything that moved. When there were no guests on the island, sometimes Ralph and I would take the large boats, the *Bahama Mama* or the *Alberta*, and go out on undersea ventures. Capt. Eric Sawyer ran the *Mama* and Johnny Cass piloted the *Alberta*, and both men knew the surrounding waters intimately. We photographed sunken ships, giant tarpon, moray eels and octopuses, and a giant whale shark, which was probably the most exciting undersea experience I will have for a long time. (More about this later.)

During my many hours under the sea, I constantly marveled at the colorful, breath-taking fishes on the reefs. One in particular, known as the marine jewel fish (Mycrospathodon chrysyrus), always fascinated me with its dazzling beauty. It is a stunning, deep blue fish with light blue spots that glisten like hundreds of brilliant jewels, and to catch a glimpse of one of these comparatively rare beauties as it sparkles in the sunlight on a shallow reef is a sight that you will never forget. I had been keeping salt water aquariums in my apartment for some time and decided to add a jewel fish to my collection. One day while on an underwater photo trip, I spotted a beautiful specimen in the shallow water beneath me. I swam back to the boat for my hand net, and then attempted to capture it. The jewel fish lives in a fortress honeycombed with powerful stinging coral, and in trying to net the elusive creature, I brushed against the coral several times. The pain is nearly unbearable and it burns the flesh; you can actually hear it sear your skin, and it is similar to placing your arm or leg up against a red-hot stove. In addition to the coral, the little beauty constantly took refuge in coral pockets inhabited by long-spined sea urchins, which look very much like a long-needled porcupine. The needles are five to eight inches long and extremely brittle. They are so sharp that they will penetrate the flesh several inches at the slightest touch and then will break off, leaving the needle inside. A quick brush against one of these urchins usually results in at least several punctures and each is as painful as a bee sting. They will go right through gloves or diving suits and abound everywhere.

A dozen coral burns and twenty urchin stings later, I had the little inch-long fish safely in my net. Total time had taken nearly two hours. It was my first jewel fish. Later, as I became more experienced, I was able to cut the time down to ten or fifteen minutes, sometimes even managing to get one in fifteen seconds, depending upon the location.

I brought the precious specimen home and added it to my aquarium. Mr. Lyon was so impressed with its fantastic beauty that he asked if I would set up an aquarium in his house. This was a project I greatly enjoyed. I set up a 30-gallon aquarium and decorated it with the choicest corals, angelfish, butterfly fish, and an assortment of marine beauties found in the Bahama waters. Later I set up a 50-gallon tank and made it even more lavish than the other. He enjoyed them both immensely and would often call all his guests together just to watch me feed the fish.

This was my start as a marine collector, for although I had collected before, and even displayed sea horses and other specimens at the Annual Flower Show in Miami, I had only done it as a part time venture. I did not realize the full potential of it until I had begun collecting in the Bahamas and then I knew I had found my life's work. I enjoyed working as a photographer and had many interesting experiences, especially when I was making movies of spectacular leaping blue marlin or underwater movies for my boss, but collecting was always in my mind, and I spent much of my free time gathering specimens for the aquariums at the big house. They were probably the most elaborately supplied salt-water aquariums in the world. I also contributed some of my specimens to the Lerner Marine Laboratory at the other end of the island, since they were always grateful to receive any pretty little fishes for their aquariums.

Time went by and I became more and more restless as a photographer. I spent most of my time cruising aboard luxury yachts in the Gulf Stream trolling for blue marlin, since an important part of my job was to photograph them as they performed their spectacular aerial exhibits. I also made movies of the angler fighting the fish and followed the story through to the boating or release of the marlin, whichever was the case. During slow days when the marlin weren't striking, I scooped up floating seaweed with a long handled net, and was always amazed at the fantastic variety of life found in this floating grass. There was likely to be anything, from baby flying fish to strange sargassum fish, a weird fish that looks exactly like the weed, even having appendages of skin simulating the weed itself. I also found baby dolphin, tuna, sea turtles, porcupine fish, sea horses, and a vast assortment of small minnows, many of which I was unable to identify. Some of the guests became so enthused with weed dipping that they even left the fishing chair to join in this interesting diversion. I kept only the most unusual specimens, and these were added to the aquarium so that Mr. Lyon could enjoy them. He never failed to find enjoyment in all the strange things that lived in the sea, and I always admired his great interest in life.

Although I immensely enjoyed being a photographer, I began to feel that life was passing me by and it seemed there was never enough time devoted to underwater movies and aqua-lung work, which was my real incentive for taking the job in the first place. I began to long for the reefs and wanted to spend all my time on them, but under the present circumstances this was impossible and the months of cruising on top of the ocean, when I yearned to be beneath it, began to tell on me. It was a burning desire, and finally when I could stand it no longer, I gave up my good job to attempt something completely insecure, but something I longed to do. I decided to be a full-time marine collector.

Reluctantly, I told Ralph and Mr. Lyon that I would like to leave, and when the plane was winging me back to Miami and a very uncertain future, I wondered if I had done the right thing. I had given up a fabulous job, but I had made up my mind that I would be a collector and had a good idea of how I would go about it. I even had picked out the name of Coral Reef Exhibits to call my collecting business, for I knew then that although I wanted to become a marine collector, my ultimate aim and love was aquariums, and eventually I hoped to build a beautiful aquarium and display the exotic, colorful gems of the sea so that everyone could enjoy their spectacular beauty.

I violated the number one skin diving rule from the very start of my marine collecting career. I nearly always dove alone. It wasn't pleasant, but it was necessary. I just could not find diving companions who could get off during the week to go with me, and I seldom worked on Sundays, so that in order to carry out my plans as a marine collector, I had to dive alone most of the time. Upon occasion I took other divers with me when I couldn't get enough fish by myself to fill my orders, and there were times when I brought along friends, relatives, scientists, and photographers. But on the whole, since I dove year round and often five or six days a week, I dove largely by myself without even anyone in the boat.

There were times when I regretted it deeply. Near accidents could easily have been prevented if I had adhered to the rules. Yet, I was determined to make a success of my collecting venture and would let absolutely nothing stand in the way, even if I had to dive alone.

Yet, it always had its advantages. A man can never feel so free as when he heads out to sea on a beautiful day and can look forward to exploring and gathering colorful little creatures on the wonderland of the coral reefs. It is a fabulous job at times, full of adventure and excitement, but it's also hard work; sometimes almost inhuman work. I can recall days of diving and fighting the sea that left me so exhausted I could hardly breathe. I would breathe long, deep breaths for hours on end even after I was home in bed.

On a typical day I would get up at 4:30 in the morning and pack a dozen or so boxes of fish for shipment to various parts of the country. After working feverishly to get them out to the airport on time, I would eat a hurried breakfast and then drive eighty miles down to the Florida Keys. There I would unload a fantastic assortment of jugs, pots, nets, buckets, and all types of collecting gear, including a heavy outboard motor and gas cans, and carry these down the dock to the boat. It takes about twenty trips back and forth to the car to get all the gear aboard. Next, I would start the motor and head out to sea. I might go as far as twenty miles before finally selecting a collecting spot. Then I would anchor the boat, put on mask and snorkle and dive all day long in water 10 to 25 feet deep. In summer I may dive ten or twelve hours at a stretch, perhaps not even coming out of the water to eat my lunch. When I finally do climb aboard the boat, it's because the sun is setting and it's getting difficult to see underwater. After pulling up the anchor and changing into dry clothes, I head back to the docks. I eat my luch on the way, and since I am now carrying a tremendous load of water in the boat, with perhaps six or eight five-gallon jugs of sea water and a half dozen or more five-gallon containers of live specimens, the trip back usually takes about three times as long as the one out. Once ashore I spend about an hour unloading the boat. I am so tired that I can hardly lift the heavy jugs of water up to the dock, especially if it is low tide and they have to be lifted up six or seven feet. Mosquitoes and sand flies descend on me by the thousands and since it is probably ten or eleven o'clock at night, there is no one to help. Somehow I get the car loaded and lift the heavy motor up onto the dock by myself. I wipe the windshield of the car clean of mosquitoes and sand flies and start the eighty-mile drive back to Miami.

When I get home it may be around midnight and I still have to unload the car and bring the fish into the shop so they can be supplied with air. I have repeated this same procedure four or five times in a row and at the end of the week I have been so utterly exhausted that I can scarcely move. Then I rest and sleep for a full day and start the new week fresh but weary. I have worked a hundred hours or more a week for many weeks at a stretch, which over the years finally paid off since I became well-known as a collector and built a reputation of dependability all over the United States.

I don't have to work as hard now as I did those first few years since I have learned so much about the ways and peculiarities of fish that I can collect a hundred times more than when I first started. I can recall the first Blue Neon Goby that I had ever caught. I had worked so hard to net that pretty little fish. Now I can dive down and net as many as twenty-five in a single dive, and with the same net I used before. It all came with experience.

I never use dynamite or poisons, and seldom use traps, but instead I catch nearly everything in small hand nets which I make to my own specifications. I have found that I can catch practically every fish on the reefs with my little nets and bring them back with scarcely a scale out of place. I tried trapping fish quite a few times and was fairly successful, but the fish often injured themselves against the wire of the traps, especially when an eel or grouper tried to get into the trap to devour them. Sometimes a trap would give a good haul but more often than not it would yield nothing but grunts, snappers, grouper, moray eels, and an occasional angelfish. I also used a trawl net for collecting grass specimens such as sea horses, cowfish, boxfish, and file-fish in the shallow bay areas. Although I had successfully caught most of these specimens with skin diving gear, it was much simpler and more practical to drag for them with a trawl net. It was also safer as they are usually found in dirty water inhabited by sharks and barracuda.

The real joy in collecting, though, is outwitting the colorful fish out on the coral reef. While it doesn't require too much skill for a diver, holding his breath, to swim down and shoot a fish with a speargun, it takes a considerable amount of effort to swim down and capture a little beauty alive in a small hand net. Bringing the fish back alive is a lot more sport than just shooting them and tossing the dead fish in the boat. When you catch them alive, the thrill of the capture is only part of the fun, for you can bring the fish home and enjoy them for months if you have an aquarium. Although I shipped most of my exotic specimens to aquariums all over the United States, I always kept a good assortment of them at home so I could observe them and learn how to better care for them. I began writing articles about them for various aquarium and pet magazines, and also wrote question and answer columns in two magazines on a monthly basis. I figured that if people didn't know how to keep the fish alive, they certainly wouldn't want to order them for their aquarium, so I did everything I could to insure their success with salt-water aquariums.

I liked collecting very much, but there were times I

In 1954 the first salt-water aquarium store in the country was opened by the author and differed from the usual fresh-water aquarium store by featuring live marine plants, exotic corals, and salt-water aquariums.

regretted shipping off beautiful fish before I had a chance to really enjoy them. Collecting was hard work, and it was much more fun catching fish for my own aquariums than collecting them for others. I began to wish that I could build a large aquarium and just catch enough fish to stock it. This way I could enjoy both ends of the collecting field.

3
The Sea Monster's
Last Voyage

THE *Sea Monster* WAS A WEIRD LOOKING CRAFT WITH ITS home-made cabin, its odd, boxlike design, and its perpetual lack of paint. Yet, despite its strange lines, it was seaworthy and gave me years of service. It could plow through a heavy sea with ease and didn't slap the water as it came down on the waves. Instead, it went right on through them.

"Straughan's Folly" was a nickname given the old boat by diving companions Tom Reed and Rick Fried. Both had advised me that any money I spent fixing up the *Sea Monster* was a waste, but I listened and painted, stating that it floated and that that was the main thing. I had taken the boat home to overhaul it, and after scraping off two full bushels of oysters that had been living on the hull for the last few years, I began to wonder whether or not they were right.

I had two boats at the time, the *Royal Empress,* which I used to work the reefs, and the *Sea Monster,* which I usually kept in the bay. One was docked in Miami and the other in Key Largo, so that I could work in either area from my own boat.

The day of the launching of the *Sea Monster* arrived
and several friends, who doubted seriously if the boat
would float after the addition of my cabin and gigantic live
wells, were on hand for the official launching. My chief
assistant, Claire Holloway, had volunteered to christen the
boat, so I wrapped a bottle of root beer for the occasion.
Among those present were Warren Prince and Ed More-
house, owner of Aquarama, a huge traveling aquarium
that I was associated with at the time. Warren wanted to

One of the author's boats, *The Sea Monster*, stands ready for
launching. It was christened with the bottle of root beer on the
bow.

go along for the ride and do a little fishing, and Ed was interested in watching me trawl for specimens.

All went well at the launching, which was done at Grant's Dock in Coconut Grove, Florida. Claire swung the

The *Sea Monster* being christened by Claire Holloway with the bottle of root beer. The weird craft gave the author some harrowing moments, one time nearly sinking due to hurricane winds. The "Monster" now rests quietly on the ocean floor.

bottle of root beer and Grant lifted the newly christened *Sea Monster* into the air on his hoist and settled it gently in the water. Much to our surprise it floated!

Claire went back to her yacht, and Warren, Ed, and myself cautiously boarded the vessel. I started the motor and we headed out to sea. It was a strange sight. I had been using the 20 gallon canning crocks for carrying specimens and with these placed on the roof of the cabin it gave the appearance from a distance of smoke stacks. Everyone laughed at us as we made our way across the busy harbor. We stopped briefly at Claire's beautiful sailing yacht the *McCaw*, and then departed for the open sea.

The boat handled fairly well except that the cabin made it extremely topheavy. We didn't notice this too much until one of us leaned over to look out of the window and the boat nearly tipped over. After that we were afraid to breathe. When we finally reached an area where I could start dragging the trawl, I decided to let some water into the live wells. I pulled out some plugs and the water gushed in with a huge spout rising nearly a foot up into the center of the boat. We all watched nervously as the boat began to fill with water, hoping it would fill the live wells sufficiently and cease coming in, but unfortunately this didn't happen. I had made the wells much too large and the boat would sink before they would fill. I quickly replaced the plugs and we bailed some of the water so that a sudden wave wouldn't capsize us. Then the trawling began. Every time I pulled in the huge net, the water in the live wells would all rush to the side of the boat I was standing upon and Warren and Ed would sit on the opposite side to keep my side from going under. If one of them got up, the boat would have quickly turned over. A strong east wind added to the discomfort and the echo of "Straughan's Folly" began to ring in my ear.

The major troubles with the craft were that the cabin caused too much wind resistance and the live wells were too large. Being covered, the wells could take in quite a bit of water before it was noticed and then the wind pushing the boat to one side could cause all the water in the wells to roll. With three men aboard the small craft, each moving independently, it was difficult to keep the boat on an even keel, making it necessary for each man to announce when he was going to stand up or move to another part of the boat.

We made it home that day, but I decided that I would have to somewhat alter the boat to make it safe. I removed the sides from the cabin so that the wind could blow through, and I took down the heavy boom, which I had originally envisioned as a labor saving device to haul in my nets. It, too, was impractical, being too top-heavy, and would have tipped the boat over before I could have dragged the nets in.

The *Sea Monster* behaved much better with the sides of the cabin removed, but the live wells were still dangerous. When they became partially filled with water, the boat would suddenly become sluggish and difficult to steer, and I immediately had to raise the covers and bail them dry to keep the boat out of danger. I thought about removing them entirely since I seldom used them except in the calmest waters, but somehow I never got around to it until it was nearly too late. In spite of the monicker "Straughan's Folly," I did get a lot of use out of the old *Sea Monster* and kept it at the Dinner Key Yacht Basin for about a year. I used it mostly in the bay where I dragged for sea horses, and it was excellent for this purpose.

On calm days I would throw over my drag net, set the motor at the proper speed, and then put on my mask and snorkle and go over the side. I would swim in back of the net sometimes holding on to the frame when I grew tired or when I wanted to observe closely just what was going into it. In this manner I could often spot sea horses that the net would otherwise miss and I would stay down as long as I could hold my breath. On several occasions, boats

in the vicinity would come in close, no doubt wondering
what the boat was doing going along by itself and I would
surface after hearing their motors and wave to them, indi-
cating that I had everything under control. I am sure they
thought I was either crazy, or a fool, or both, but I found
this practice both profitable, interesting, and comfortable.
On hot days it became quite miserable sitting in the boat
all day and so I started my underwater escapades with the
net. It also provided me with information on how the net
behaved under water, how the fish behaved when the net
approached them and, in addition, I could lift the net over
any damaging obstacles, so that all in all it was a good idea.
There was one danger, though, and that was if the rope
hauling the trawl broke. I would have to swim to the boat
immediately, otherwise, without the burden of the net, the
boat would speed up and I would be left behind. Since I
nearly always worked alone, I depended on no one and
always kept this in mind.

I did many foolhardy things in my early collecting days.
One time I tried dragging my trawl in seventy-five feet of
water out along the edge of the Gulf Stream at dusk. I
went over the side and swam down fifty or sixty feet, trying
to see how the net was behaving in the subdued light. This
was really dangerous, for I was right next to very deep
water heavily infested with sharks, and also there was a
strong current so that if the trawl line had broken, I would
have had a very difficult time getting back to the boat by
myself. Besides, it was in a remote area where there probably would not be another boat along for a week or more.
Luckily the line held and I climbed back into the boat
deciding that this was not a very sensible thing to do. I
pulled in the net and found that for all my trouble the net
held nothing more spectacular than a host of scorpion fish

and octopuses. Still, it was a strange haul from such deep water.

Everyone is always interested in what comes up in the trawl net. It is sort of like nature's grab-bag. You never really know what you will catch. It's always a thrill to spot the big sea horses in the net as you first unfold it in the boat. There is likely to be anything from baby nurse sharks to spiny boxfish, cowfish, trunkfish, filefish, pipefish, starfish, toadfish, and many others. I work in reverse from the shrimp fishermen. What they regard as "trash" is what I collect, and I seldom bother with the shrimp since I am too busy looking out for my live specimens. Catching the specimens is only a small part of the battle. The rest is in keeping them alive until they can be marketed and shipped. This usually takes a lot of doing.

For this type of work, the *Sea Monster* was perfect. Despite the fact that she was not a beautiful boat by any stretch of the imaginaion, she had her good points. She didn't leak a drop and she was reasonably light so that in a calm sea she would travel at a fair pace, and in a rough sea she was like a duck, bobbing in and out of the waves with scarcely a drop landing on her hull. When the old docks were torn down at Dinner Key, Warren Prince and myself loaded the *Monster* with food and drink and cruised nearly fifty miles south to another docking area in lower Biscayne Bay. Storm warnings were up that day and the seas were rainy and choppy, yet the old *Sea Monster* made it in good time and with no trouble whatever. I began to even feel slightly proud of her.

I rented a new dock space and used the boat for collecting in the South Bay area, taking it out to the ocean when the weather was good. This was a long, lonely trip and usually averaged about forty miles, much of it over open water. I made the trip quite a few times, without too much

I collected the bizarre spiny boxfish with a dragnet or sometimes by hand on the grass flats. Though fearsome in appearance, they are quite harmless except for their bite.

trouble and I began to like the old *Sea Monster* more and more.

A typical day in my collecting career began with the weather report of moderate winds and clear skies. The winds were moderate allright, at least when I started out. It was blowing about 15 m.p.h., which would make rather rough seas way out, so I decided to head for some off-shore islands and work in the lee of them. These islands were in a remote area and were approximately eighteen miles from the docks. Most of the trip was across open, unprotected waters. I used the venerable old *Sea Monster* for the trip and it was a relatively smooth crossing. Soon, I was in the protected waters of the islands and, as I had expected, it was quite calm in the lee side and suitable for collecting. I chose a likely area and dove in the shallow, inshore gorgonia patches and had a fairly successful day. Among my catch were numerous black angelfish, beau gregories, least and four-eyed butterfly fish, and a few assorted demoiselles. It wasn't a good haul but in view of the fact that the water was extremely riled up and dirty in most areas, it was certainly better than nothing. The sun started getting low on the horizon and I decided to head for home.

I ate my lunch as I headed through the narrow mangrove channels that led through the islands and secured the collecting jugs and other gear in preparation for the crossing. I knew it would be quite rough for I had noticed that the wind had picked up considerably as the day progressed. I had, however, crossed this wide expanse of water many times, and assumed this would be just another miserable, wet, and rough four-hour ordeal. When I finally reached the open sea, a terrific gust of wind nearly turned the boat around as it caught me by surprise. Huge waves were crashing into the narrow protected mangrove channel and I knew at a glance that this would be a very rough crossing. The wind was blowing about 50 to 60 m.p.h. and the sea was whipped into a churning white mass of towering waves. For a moment I considered camping on the island, but then I thought that since my family expected me home that night I would cause them considerable worry; I decided to head across. It was extremely rough and although I was progressing only a mile or two an hour, at least I was making headway. I decided to head straight across, since this way land was only about six miles away. Then, I could cruise along the shore and head south until I reached the docks. This would be longer, but at least I would be heading into the wind rather than going through the big waves sideways. All went well for the first hour or two. The wind blew fiercely and the waves plowed into the boat in rapid succession. Many huge torrents of water struck the bow and went clear over the roof of the cabin, landing fifteen or twenty feet behind the boat. At times there would be a succession of nine- and ten-foot waves, numbering a half dozen or more, at a time. These would be so close together that one would break directly over the boat while the other was hitting the bow. It was quite frightening for it was impossible to miss them. The old *Sea Monster* was taking a terrible beating and I hoped she didn't break apart under the constant pounding. I wore my sun glasses to keep the salt out of my eyes for I was completely drenched almost as soon as I had left shore. Despite the extremely rough seas, my spirits were high, for I had no idea of the serious trouble that was soon to confront me, and I knew was gaining on the opposite shore.

The waves were still tremendous and I knew the boat had taken on water, but in my constant battle with the sea, and in my cold and wet condition I had no idea how much I had taken aboard. I was too absorbed with keeping the boat in line with the huge waves to notice what was going on in the boat. Finally, I felt confident that the worst was over, for land was only a mile away. I felt amost jubilant. Then, suddenly I noticed that the boat seemed a little sluggish. It didn't respond very well to the controls. At first I attributed this to the rough seas and the current. At any rate I wasn't alarmed about it. Then, I noticed that the bow had a definite list to one side. It was quite pronounced and I knew that there was a lot of water in the wells. However, since I was so near shore, I felt certain I could make it, as I knew it would be difficult to bail and still keep the boat headed into the waves. Huge waves continued to pound on the old *Monster's* bow and I suddenly realized that the bow was no longer rising after a wave had passed. The stern was higher than the bow and it was almost impossible to steer. "My God, I'm sinking," I hollered aloud. I swung the boat around so that I was heading with the waves and opened the throttle wide to see if I could bring the bow back up. It was no use! Even running with the waves, the bow continued to settle down into the depths. To my utter horror I watched the water slowly pour into the boat. A huge wave caught the boat and turned it sideways and it was completely out of control. The motor wouldn't move it. Already the water was up to the top of the seats and the boat was settling like an old tin can thrown into the water. In trying to raise the bow, I had headed back out to sea and was now about three or four miles from shore. The boat was wallowing at the mercy of the seas when a desperate idea struck me. I had been carrying four five gallon jugs of fresh sea water in the bow, and I realized that they were weighting the bow down considerably. If I could throw them overboard, the reduction in weight might possibly keep the boat up long enough for me to bail out some of the water. It was a desperate measure with seconds at stake, for already the boat was on its way down. I straightened the boat with the waves as much as I could and stumbled forward into the bow. This had to be done quickly, for I knew my added weight in the bow would practically sink the boat. I reached forward and quickly grabbed the first jug with a mighty heave. So quickly did I wrench it from the deck that it flew apart covering the deck with glass. I grabbed another jug and heaved it over the side. Time was so precious that I couldn't dodge the sharp glass fragments and I felt them grinding into my bare feet as I fought to maintain balance in the turbulent sea. By some miracle the boat stayed afloat long enough for me to wrestle the two remaining jugs into the stern of the boat. I figured their added weight in the stern would help level the boat. A tremendous wave caught the poor *Monster* sideways and I leaned far out over the sea in the opposite direction, trying to keep the tired old boat from capsizing. This was the closest yet I had come to tipping over and one side of the boat actually took on water. Another inch and the old *Sea Monster* would have been gone forever. With the water just out of the bow, the boat seemed a little more level.

I had turned the motor down to idle when the boat was no longer under control, and during the dreadful few minutes of near disaster, she was at the mercy of the sea. I began furiously bailing water with a large plastic waste basket. This dipped up five gallons at a time and soon I had most of the water out of the bow. Things began to look a little better and I began to get faint hope that she wouldn't sink after all. The bow had lifted considerably with all the weight gone, and I once more opened the motor to full throttle. I headed with the wind again and opened the rear drain plugs to let the water out of the stern. Then when the boat was buoyant, I turned around once more and headed for land.

I had to fight my way through the monstrous seas once more, this time with the constant fear that the same thing would happen again. My feet were badly cut and I didn't dare look at them; there was still several inches of water in the boat so that they were constantly submerged. This eased the pain considerably, and since I figured that I couldn't do anything about them anyhow, I would not look at them until I reached shore. To add to the peril, I struck something under water and feared that I had sheared a pin in the motor. It would be almost impossible to repair a pin in these rough seas, but the pin held and I tried not to put any extra strain on it. Then I noticed that I was almost out of fuel. The constant maneuvering and deceleration necessary in a heavy sea had nearly exhausted my fuel supply. I had an extra two gallons in a separate container but I didn't want to use it until I reached shore, since I still had a fifteen-mile trip back to the docks. I worried about the shear pin and the fuel and headed grimly through the seas, each wave smashing into my face so that I was half blinded. I had discarded my sunglasses during the emergency.

Suddenly, something struck a fierce blow in my face and nearly knocked me out of the boat. My head went numb and when I took my hand down from my face, it was covered with blood. A piece of the cabin roof, which had been weakened by the constant pounding, had broken loose and had struck me square in the face at a tremendous speed. My face was completely numb and I felt for gashes so I could stop the bleeding. I began to feel this was my day of doom, for not only did I have to keep the boat constantly in line with the waves, but I also had to worry about the busted shear pin and whether the gas would hold out. Now I was wounded! I couldn't find any open gashes, and as the pain grew more intense, I decided that I had been hit square in the mouth. I ran my fingers over my teeth several times to see if they were all still there and spit blood for at least an hour. It was maddening! I didn't have any way of telling how badly I had been hurt. I had to keep the boat under control and the waves kept lashing at my face. The boat took a slight lurch as it had before. This time, however, with the weight out of the bow, there was much less danger and slowly I gained on the shore. It seemed to take a million years to cover that last quarter of a mile. I thought I would never get to the safety of the land and the boat seemed to crawl the last few hundred feet. Finally I made it.

I ran the boat right up onto the beach and then took stock of the damage. My mouth had stopped bleeding and I could feel a nasty open gash in my lip. It was terribly swollen. My feet had also stopped bleeding and I washed them in the cleaner water near shore so that I could inspect them. They were both a mass of cuts, but fortunately, none were very deep. I washed them as well as I could and let them dry before putting on my socks, which I figured would keep the dirt out of the wounds. Then I bailed out all the water from the bow and stern. I opened the front live well and it was filled right to the top. The water cascading over the cabin roof had completely filled it. This, added to the water in the bow, had nearly sunk the boat. I emptied the water from the well and secured all the gear for the return trip back to the docks. I had to refill the fish containers, for during the ordeal they had nearly emptied themselves from the constant sloshing about, and the fish were swimming on their sides. Then, after I had rested awhile, and calmed my nerves, I started back. The wind was still very strong but the waves were much smaller as I was now in a more protected area, and since the boat was empty of excess water, it handled well so that I made it back to the docks without further mishap.

When I finally reached shore, I was using up the last drops of gas and was battered and bruised from head to foot. I began to realize what a narrow escape from disaster I had had and what a predicament I would have been in had the boat sunk. I would have been tossed into a very rough sea with little hope of rescue. Most likely I could have made it to shore, but even then I would have been at least fifteen miles from the nearest house and would have had to wander through impenetrable mangrove wilderness back to civilization. It would have been a terrible ordeal, especially since I was barefoot with nothing but swim trunks for clothes. The mosquitoes would have eaten me alive and my feet would have been cut to ribbons along the sharp coral coastline. Also, I would have lost my boat, collecting nets, and all of my gear. Actually, if I had tried to reach the dock where I had left the car by walking along the shoreline, it would have been a nearly impossible feat. The distance probably would have been over a hundred miles because I would have had to walk in the bays and out along the peninsulas of the irregular coastline. Now that I think of it, I probably would have attempted swimming the fifteen miles rather than trying to walk along the shore.

I unloaded the boat, put on my clothes, and headed back to Miami. It felt so good to be alive that I sang as I started for home. But even on shore, I was far from safe as I soon came to realize. As if the terrible ordeal at sea was not enough, I had barely left the dock on my way to Miami when I was confronted with an equally dangerous situation. It seemed that the perils of this day would never end. The road back to civilization from the ocean was an old, seldom used road in much need of repair. There was nothing for fifteen miles except a canal on each side with no homes, lights, or buildings of any kind. It was a lonely drive and I always felt a little relieved when I finally made it back to the highway. On one stretch in particular, there was an extremely bad place where the pavement had caved in and the road was so badly torn up that in order to pass it a driver had to slow down almost to the point of stopping.

It was just about dusk as I traveled over the lonely road that day, and as I looked ahead, I caught a glimpse of a car half hidden in the bushes, right at the bad area. I had always thought that this would be an ideal place for a holdup since robbers would know that anyone passing on the road would have to slow down almost to a stop to get by. Also, because there was nothing for miles in any direction, a victim would have little help from passersby. The thought of robbers struck me immediately as I approached the bad section of road, and when I got there I stared in disbelief as the machine in the bushes suddenly pulled across the road, blocking my path. There were three men in the car and one held a small gun, probably an automatic. I stopped my car and one of the robbers got out and started walking toward me. I didn't have any money with me, and I knew that they would probably kill me and that I would never be found in that desolate area, so I decided to take a desperate chance. I began to back up as fast as I could.

Suddenly, I noticed another car in my mirror. It appeared from nowhere, but had probably been hiding in the bushes. He swung across the road in back of me so that I could not get away. I was completely boxed in and the canal was on both sides so I could not run off the road. I decided to ram the car in front of me and then jump into the canal and escape in the confusion. Darkness had almost set in and I felt that if I rammed the car, perhaps the crooks at least would be apprehended as they would have no way to get off the narrow road. Also, since I had collision insurance, my car could be fixed without too much expense. I stopped backing up and put the car in second. Then I headed for the car in front of me at top speed. Apparently they read my thoughts, for as I approached them, they pulled their car out of the road and almost went into the canal. I roared past them holding my head down as much as I could, expecting them to shoot at me, and pushed the throttle to the floor. It was dark now and I could see their headlights pursuing me, but I left them far behind. I had a new Plymouth with a V-8 engine and I went over a 110 m.p.h. on that old, broken-down road.

When I got to Homestead, I frantically called the police. They said they couldn't go down there as it was out of their jurisdiction, but they suggested that I go back and see if I could get the robbers' license number. I was furious and told them not to leave the station, as they might hurt themselves. Then I called the highway patrol. They said it was also out of their patrol area. Thoroughly disgusted, I hung up and drove on home.

It was quite a day! I never took the *Sea Monster* out again after that. The fact that I had almost drowned in the lonely seas, combined with the near robbery, made me shun the area for years to come, and the *Sea Monster* slowly rotted away at the docks. Finally, I wrote a letter to the dock owner and told him he could have her, but she was in such poor condition that he finally towed her away from the docks and let her settle to the bottom where she would make a home for the fish. When I heard about this a few years later, I agreed that the best place for the old boat was at the bottom of the sea. She had met her final resting place.

4
Personal Encounters with Sharks

IN THE PAST TEN YEARS, I HAVE ENCOUNTERED NEARLY every form of life in the sea including hammerhead sharks, tiger sharks, makos, giant manta rays, and, on one occasion, a giant whale shark that weighed over fifteen tons, not to mention several thousand moray eels and giant barracuda. Since I nearly always dive alone, and often stray quite far from my small boat, my meetings with the predators of the sea are often quite eventful since hungry sharks, who normally would have stayed at a safe distance had I been accompanied by other divers, became particularly curious.

My first encounter with a dangerous shark occurred in the shallows at North Key Largo, Florida. I had waded out from shore and was swimming along in the shallow water looking for shells and colorful fish. My companions were my wife Rosemary and her girl friend, Jeanette Goodreau, a shapely blonde with a keen interest in marine life, and Nina, my Labrador Retriever, whom I had trained to dive with me. We were about a quarter mile from shore when the pleasure of a beautiful day was badly shaken by

Sand tiger shark (Carcharias taurus) swims in very shallow sandy areas, and has a mouthfull of sharp, pointed teeth that protrude outward in an evil manner. Although it feeds largely on fish, it could attack a diver, especially if he was swimming in a school of fish—a dangerous habit. (Photos courtesy Marineland Studios, Marineland, Florida)

Head-on view of the Sand Tiger as it would appear when heading toward the unhappy skindiver.

(Photo courtesy Marineland of Florida)

Remoras or sharksuckers attached to a Sand Tiger Shark. Remoras swimming free in the water are almost a certain sign of a shark in the area, for they often leave their host and guide him to a prospective meal so they can feed on leftovers.

(Photo courtesy Marineland of Florida)

the presence of a large, ugly shark. Nina had just left the innertube, which I towed along with us so that she could rest when necessary, and was swimming a short distance ahead. The shark was over twice my length and its huge eyes, protruding from the end of its weird mallet shaped head, were looking me over carefully no doubt appraising me for gastronomical purposes. We swam along together each looking at the other with a fierce expression, although I must admit that the shark's expression was more frightening than my own, and when we had covered several hundred feet, the shark gradually eased ahead. At first I thought the ordeal was over and was quite relieved, until I realized that the shark was no longer interested in me, but was heading straight for my dog! Poor Nina was happily swimming along, completely unaware that silent death was just a few feet beneath her, and as I looked up and saw the little black feet kicking pitifully through the clear water, I suddenly became very angry. I swam right up to the shark and passed him, so that now I was between him and my dog and I thrashed, kicked and yelled in one frantic moment. The big shark stopped his assault on the dog and turned to face me, opening his mouth so that his jagged, saw-like teeth were clearly visible, and I lost my bravery immediately. He turned very sharply in a tight circle and for a few minutes we milled about the shallow water like two wrestlers about to engage in battle, except that I was very willing to leave. I had no protection whatever, not even a knife and since Nina still didn't realize what was going on, I couldn't count on her for help. I did the only thing I could under the circumstances and that was to appear the aggressor, for this would put the shark on the defensive. I made a few quick dives in the general direction of my opponent, kicking my feet strongly as I did, but taking care that I did not in any way block the creature's path for this would have been disastrous. The bluff apparently worked, for after a few dives, I noticed that we were getting farther apart and I didn't close the distance so the shark could swim away undisturbed. Then I placed Nina on the innertube and towed her to shore. Jeanette had put on her mask and had also seen the shark at close range. We discontinued diving for the day. It certainly was strange how the big shark had appeared out of nowhere in shallow

Sandbar shark (Eulamia milberti) is one of the most common inshore sharks and is often encountered by skin divers. It can be recognized by its high dorsal fin and can be dangerous in dirty water. (Photo courtesy Marine Studios, Marineland, Florida)

water where you could easily see a quarter of a mile around you in each direction by standing on a rock, but it shows that sharks are unpredictable and will appear where you least expect them.

Another encounter with a hammerhead shark occurred in almost the same area. It was a very gloomy day, and although it wasn't actually raining, the skies were very dark. It was the kind of day I dread when I have to dive, for when the skies are overcast, the sea becomes a dreary place. Visibility is usually poor, and diving is especially dangerous because under these conditions a man's arm or leg flashing in the dark water could easily be mistaken for a fish by some hungry shark or barracuda. Also, because of the poor visibility, it is extremely difficult to see a shark or barracuda even when they are only a few yards away. Often all that is visible of the unwanted visitor is an eye, which seems to be traveling through the water by itself, the rest of the fish being almost completely invisible.

I pondered these thoughts as I headed out to sea, and when I finally arrived at the reefs, I sat in the boat for a long while getting up the courage to go into the water. There was one consolation, however; the sea was dead calm and it would be good diving if only the sun would come out. I stood up in the bow of the boat to look around and marveled at the glossy surface of the quiet sea. It was so calm that the slightest ripple could be seen a long way off. As I stood watching the peaceful view, I suddenly noticed a large disturbance several hundred feet away. I watched for a few minutes and when it came closer, I could see that it was the dorsal fin of a shark, and a very large one at that, for the fin stuck out of the water a full two feet. It appeared to be on the prowl for food, for it would swim back and forth in a regular pattern in such a way that it would take in a wide area, covering it very effectively. At times it would quicken its pace, perhaps to survey some prospective meal, and then it would slow down to its original speed. As it came closer to the boat, I became aware of its tremendous size. Its huge dorsal fin had been out of the water so long that it was completely dry from the warm air, and the high tail which also protruded above the surface gave the impression of two sharks until I saw that it was just one very large hammerhead shark, the largest I had ever seen! It was at least 17 feet long. I watched the giant creature for about a half-hour until it finally eased below

Lemon shark (Negaprion brevirostris) is a very active, shallow water shark common in tropical waters and dangerous under the proper conditions. It is a pale yellowish brown in color and is very swift when aroused. It often approaches a diver from behind, scurrying away at top speed (you hope) when discovered. (Photo courtesy Marine Studios, Marineland, Florida)

the surface and quietly disappeared into the gloomy water. It took me a long time to get into my rubber diving suit that day and even then I sat in the boat and wondered if I should take a chance and dive. I finally got up courage and went into the water, but I didn't swim very far from the boat. Fortunately, I didn't see the big fish any more, but I suspect he saw me and perhaps looked me over once or twice while I was busy chasing a small Angelfish into my net. He may have stayed out of range so I couldn't see him and it was just as well that he did.

A few weeks later, I saw another big hammerhead shark in the shallow sand flats quite close to shore. I was in the boat this time on my way out to the reefs. As I passed by the shark, I thought about the time a hammerhead had attacked my dog, so I decided to give this one a scare. In the other encounter, the battle was fought in the shark's element where he had all the advantages, now we were each in our own element and the contest was more fair. I headed for the shark at top speed and ran along side him, forcing him gradually into very shallow water so that he could barely swim. His back and dorsal fin were completely out of water and I took advantage of this by hitting him on the head several times with an oar. This so enraged him that he lifted his huge bulk half way out of the water in an attempt to bite me, but I kept well out of range of the vicious mouth. I gave him several more good clouts and he finally squirmed back into the deeper water and swam quickly away. I figured that this time I had frightened at least one shark to repay them for the many times they had frightened me.

Tiger sharks are one of the most short tempered and aggressive sharks in the sea. They are also very common in tropical waters. Skindivers should give them a wide berth if they encounter one, in or out of the boat. There are numerous records where these large, powerful creatures have attacked boats. One of my encounters adds to the record.

It was a beautiful clear day, perfect for diving and I hurriedly loaded the boat and headed out for the reefs. The water was a flat, glassy calm, a rare day at sea, and

Another view of the lemon shark showing that both dorsal fins are about the same size. Notice the remoras attached to the shark. They will also fasten themselves to skin divers. If a large remora suddenly appears out of the blue and swims around you, it is a good indication that a shark is close by. (Photo courtesy Marine Studios, Marineland, Florida)

soon I reached my collecting area and was looking around for a suitable area to begin work. I had just picked out a reef when I noticed what appeared to be a smaller reef off to one side; except that it began to move. It was a huge tiger shark! In the past year I had read of nearly a dozen shark attacks, some fatal, and I no longer relished tempting

Bull shark or cub shark (Carcharhinus leucas) is another shark likely to be encountered by the diver in shallow water. It is a powerful aggressive shark likely to be dangerous when feeding. The author has encountered them on the reefs while collecting and they show little fear of man. (Photo courtesy Marine Studios, Marineland, Florida)

fate by diving in the water with this monster, especially since I was alone.

I decided to drive the creature out of the area so I could dive in peace. I headed directly for the creature at top speed and soon had it quite worried. Each time it turned, I would follow with the boat, but after ten or fifteen minutes I found that we were going nowhere. The huge shark was swimming in large circles so I wasn't accomplishing a thing. I knew it was a tiger shark since I had had plenty of opportunity to observe it in the clear water. I jabbed at it several times with the end of my long handled dip net, but still it refused to leave the vicinity. It was a perfect day and I wanted to get into the water, but I continued following the shark. The water was about ten feet deep and I estimated the shark to be approximately fourteen feet long; it was simple to compute his size when the boat passed over him. I was beginning to wonder if the shark was ever going to leave when it suddenly changed its tactics.

It stopped swimming and began slowly circling the boat. It was huge and seemed to be about three feet in diameter. I could clearly see its sharp teeth when it opened its jaws wide several times as if to frighten me. It was an evil looking creature. Since the water was glassy calm, it could see me as plainly as I could see it, and it swam around the boat at an angle tipping its head upward as if to study me. Suddenly, without warning, it swam off about fifteen or twenty feet, turned sharply and headed straight for the boat! It hit the boat right in the center and lifted the rear end completely out of the water, motor and all. I very nearly went overboard, his attack taking me by surprise. I stood in the boat shaking and holding onto the sides expecting another attack any minute, but none came. The creature had vanished. I quickly lifted the floorboards to see if the boat was leaking, but it wasn't, and I was thankful that the bottom was half-inch plywood instead of quarter-inch, or else the huge brute would have gone clean through. There is no doubt in my mind that he actually tried to knock me overboard.

I waited in the boat for about a half hour scanning the horizon to be certain he was gone and finally got up courage to go into the water. The first thing I looked at was the

Tiger shark (Galeocerdo cuvier) has a large mouth and alert eyes. It is very large and very dangerous. The author has encountered them on various diving trips and one time was threatened by a huge, twenty-foot monster that swooped down on him out of the gloom. (Photo courtesy Marine Studios, Marineland, Florida)

Diver's view of a Bull Shark as he would confront it in deep water.
It is fearless and bold and will give no quarter.

(Photo courtesy Marineland of Florida)

A huge tiger shark lunging at food, showing its huge mouth, which could take a bite from you the size of a watermelon.

(Photo courtesy Marineland of Florida)

bottom of the boat where the shark had hit with his back. He had gone clear through the heavy Fiberglas coating and part way into the wood and had torn a large area over a foot in diameter. There were also smaller abrasions in the general area. Fiberglas is extremely tough, so I realized that he must have given the boat a tremendous wallop to go through the glass cloth as he did. Besides, the boat weighed well over a thousand pounds and he had lifted the stern end clear out of the water. I was thankful he didn't strike the motor because he surely would have destroyed it.

I was quite nervous all that day as I dove, for I kept expecting a return visit from the huge creature and I would have been terrified if I had met him in the water. I imagined he was quite aggravated and would attack anyone in the water without further provocation. Fortunately, I didn't see him again, but it taught me a lesson about bothering large sharks even from a boat. I had heard of sharks attacking boats, but never expected it to happen to me.

The nurse shark or carpet shark is one of the most common sharks in the southern coastal waters. It is usually regarded as completely harmless, but this is definitely untrue. Yet the popular trend has been to regard this creature as a plaything; a fish to be ridden underwater by any adventurous skindiver. Magazine articles and books pertaining to sharks often relate what great sport it is to ride on the back of a nurse shark, and while this can be fun when the shark behaves, it is not quite so amusing when the shark turns and attacks its rider. Contrary to popular belief, the nurse shark can bite. It has extremely powerful jaws, and although the teeth are very small, it can tear off large chunks of flesh with its rasping mouth. It doesn't bite off chunks of flesh like other sharks, but instead tears muscle and skin loose from the body, inflicting severe and painful damage. There are many authentic cases where nurse sharks have turned on a diver causing painful wounds. In the December 1954 issue of *Skin Diver* magazine, two skindivers report an encounter with a supposedly harmless nurse shark. They had been informed that the nurse shark's mouth was too small to bite with and decided to capture the creature. One of them speared it in the gills and the shark became so enraged that it attacked its tormentors. It grabbed one of them by the calf, removing a piece of flesh three inches in diameter and a half inch thick. Then it attacked the other fellow,

Nurse shark (Ginglymostoma cirratum) is one of the first sharks usually sighted by the skin diver. They like to hide under large coral heads or under ledges. Although usually considered harmless, the author recommends that divers leave the larger specimens alone. They are quick tempered and can easily tear a huge chunk of flesh from a diver with their rasping mouths. (Photo courtesy Marine Studios, Marineland, Florida)

grabbing him so firmly by the knee cap that it had to be killed before it would turn loose. One fellow required twenty-three stitches in his leg and was on crutches for a week. The shark that did all this damage was less than five feet long and weighed a mere thirty-four pounds.

While I lived in the Bahamas, I often encountered nurse sharks in caves and many of them were over eight feet long. I considered it quite sporty to sneak up to them quietly and twist their tail. They would rear about angrily and then swim madly away. I did this many times to amuse guests who went snorkling with me, but later I discontinued the practice as mounting evidence proved the fish to be dangerous. One time in particular I swam into a cave fifty or sixty feet deep that had a narrow exit at one end. It was filled with perhaps twenty or more large nurse sharks all resting quietly in the semi-darkness. I was with a companion who had never before encountered a shark and thought this would be a good time to introduce him to the creatures. I told my friend I was going to swim through the cave from the narrow end and instructed him to wait at the entrance. I didn't mention the sharks as I wanted to surprise him. When we were in position, I took a good breath and swam down into the shark filled chasm. I began twisting tails and pushing sharks in every direction but most of them were reluctant to leave. Finally, I managed to push eight or ten of them out in front of me and followed them out of the cave. My friend was laughing. He said he had been counting sharks and didn't know when they would stop coming out. When I recall the incident now, I wonder why I wasn't bitten.

I often collect small nurse sharks for pet dealers and public aquariums as they live well in captivity and make an interesting pet. My usual procedure is to grab the little fellows firmly in back of the head and swim back to the boat with them. It's as simple as that. However, sometimes there are complications. One winter I needed a small shark for a public aquarium and hadn't seen any little specimens

Side view of nurse shark taken at Marine Studios. (Photo courtesy Marine Studios, Marineland, Florida)

for a long while. I had about given up hope when I spotted one just the right size under a ledge. The water was very cold and my legs were beginning to cramp, so I decided to catch the little fellow quickly and return to the boat. I was so cold I didn't even bother to look around. I grabbed the shark by the head and was about to extract it when suddenly I felt a sharp pain in my hand. Then I saw a large green coil right in front of my face and I knew that because of my carelessness, I had been bitten by a green moray eel! I held on to the shark and the pain increased. Fortunately I had grabbed the shark with my left hand so that with my free right hand I was able to poke the eel's body with a sharp pipe I carry for such emergencies. Much to my surprise, the eel let go and disappeared behind the ledge and I returned to the surface still holding the prized fish. I had been wearing gloves which had given me sufficient protection to keep the wound from being serious. It amounted to a series of deep punctures, which I squeezed to encourage bleeding, and it quickly healed. However, if I had jerked my hand free instead of prodding the eel, it would have made a jagged wound, for the eel would not have let go.

Another interesting episode I had with a small nurse shark also occurred during the cold winter months. I needed a small specimen, and finally saw a tiny tail protruding from the edge of a large piece of coral. I swam quietly down and, since I could see only about two inches of the creature's tail, I decided to grab that and pull it out far enough so that I could grab the creature by the head. I got myself in position, grabbed the tiny tail, and pulled with all my strength. Imagine my surprise when I found that I was holding an eight-foot shark by the tail! Fortunately, it couldn't turn completely around under the coral because of lack of room, and I finally released it after it had calmed down. It swam away, giving me a very nasty look, and I learned that I should always see both ends of a shark before determining its size. The small pointed tail certainly had fooled me.

In the Bahamas sharks are very plentiful. It is not uncommon to see several of them at one time circling you at different levels when you enter the water on a deep reef. It gives one a feeling of despair to see a large shark swimming around your boat a hundred feet above, especially if you are alone, for you know you must go by him sooner or

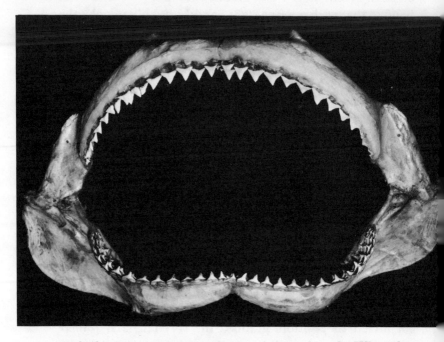

A shark's jaw contains several rows of serrated teeth. When they grab their victim, they often twist and tear away huge chunks of flesh.

later to return to the boat. For some reason they do not seem to approach as close when you are wearing an aqualung as they do when you are snorkling near the surface. Perhaps the bubbles keep them at bay, or perhaps after quick observance they realize that a skindiver must return to the surface for air and, therefore, is more vulnerable. At

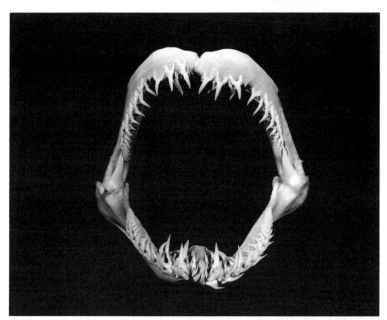

Jaws of the sand tiger shark, showing formidable teeth. Shark jaws make an attractive addition to the den or library and are easily prepared by scraping the flesh from the bone like cartilage after the jaws have been cut loose from the shark. They are then salted and dried. (Photo courtesy Marineland of Florida)

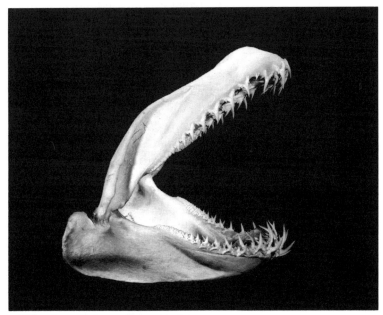

Side view of the well-prepared jaws.
(Photo courtesy Marineland of Florida)

any rate, meeting them under the sea is seldom pleasant. When you stare into their cold, zombie-like eyes, you wonder what goes on in their head. Do they regard you as another shark or as a porpoise, or worst of all, do they regard you as a slow, cumbersome, defenseless turtle? These thoughts go through your mind when the steel-gray body of a shark glides effortlessly through the water in your direction. Swimming at your top speed, the shark can keep up with you by merely coasting. When he decides to add speed, your eye can scarecely follow his swift movement through the water.

One of the few times I was actually attacked by a really dangerous shark occurred in the Bahamas. I had collected my day's catch and decided to shoot some food fish for the native who had taken me to the reefs. I shot a few grouper and had just returned to the water when I noticed a shark circling me some distance away. The water was very clear and, as he was at least seventy feet away, I didn't pay much attention to him and continued my search for fish. After I had made a few dives, I turned around suddenly under water and saw the tail end of the shark heading rapidly away. He had swum in very close when my back was turned and, due to this surprise maneuver, I became quite concerned. I swam cautiously to the surface and spun around in time to see the shark rapidly circling me again. Then, without warning, he swam straight towards me, coming so fast that I didn't see him again until his nose bumped my chest. As I was wearing face mask and snorkle, I had to stay at the surface while, for at least five minutes, the shark and I faced each other from a short distance apart. He came less than a foot away so that I could easily count his teeth. I had a double Arbalette spear gun with me at the time and I kept the spear pointed straight down his throat. The boat was at least a couple hundred feet away and the native

apparently hadn't realized my predicament until it was
nearly over. I didn't dare shoot and would have done so
only if the shark had made one final lunge. As the minutes
passed, I could tell the shark was very alert for it kept its
exact position despite the fact that there was a strong current. Its mouth was open and its cold, staring eyes watched
my every move. Finally, after what seemed a long time, I
noticed that we had drifted a few feet apart. I didn't want
to appear frightened, so I swam towards the shark, closing
the distance. This seemed to outrage it, and for a minute it
looked like it was going to bite me. I almost squeezed the
trigger on my spear gun but I am glad I didn't, for a few
minutes later it seemed that I had won the battle of nerves.
We were again separated by a distance of several feet. This
time I kicked madly and headed straight for the shark. To
my relief, it turned tail and I finally chased it from the
vicinity. It was a mako shark, a specie which is extremely
fast and quite dangerous. I had been diving in about forty
feet of water at the time, but the water became much
deeper a short way out, being as I was right near the edge
of the Gulf Stream. When I finally got back into the boat,
the native grinned and said he had seen the whole thing
but didn't know what to do about it.

A much more harrowing experience occurred off the
coast of Florida. There had been several weeks of very
stormy weather and I was getting far behind on my fish
orders. Finally, there was a reasonably calm day and I
headed out to sea for a collecting trip. I was by myself and
when I came to a likely looking area, I threw out the
anchor, put on my diving gear, and went over the side.
Again, I had only face mask and snorkle, but this time I
had no spear gun for protection since they had been out-
lawed (unfairly) in the Florida Keys. Instead, I carried a
small butterfly-type hand net about a foot long, and a short

piece of rod which I use to move sea urchins out of the
way. I was very enthused and was making a good catch
and hadn't given the slightest thought to sharks. I was
working in about twenty-five feet of water and although
the water was quite murky due to the windy weather, I
could see allright once I was on the bottom. I would take
several good breaths and then dive so that I could spend
enough time on the bottom to locate a colorful fish and
then chase him into the net before returning to the surface. I was visited by the usual number of curious barracuda but paid no attention to them as I see them nearly
every time I go out. After one especially long dive I was
resting on the surface getting my breath when I saw a
shark directly under me. I watched it for a few minutes,
then, determined that nothing was going to interfere with
my collecting, I took a deep breath and dove down upon
it. It was a small mako about seven or eight feet long! I
swam noisily towards it, giving it plenty of time to see me
and, as I approached it closely, I yelled through my
mouthpiece. It must have really been frightened because it
took off so fast that it made a huge cloud of mud when its
tail swirled near the bottom. I returned to the surface for
air and then resumed my collecting. About five minutes
later, I noticed that the shark was back again. I let it swim
around for a little while until it became quite brave and
then chased it furiously and followed it for at least sixty or
seventy feet under water. This time I figured I had chased
it away for good and I resumed my collecting.

All went well for about an hour or so, until I got a
glimpse of a shark turning away from me as I surfaced
from a dive. The way it had sneaked up on me made me
very angry and I decided to hit it on the head and this time
scare it away permanently. I floated on the surface for a
few minutes building up my breath and then noticed the

shark directly under me. This time, I would really scare it, I thought. I took a good breath and made a surface dive straight down. What an evil surprise I had! This wasn't the same shark at all, but a gigantic monster! I was practically on its back before I noticed its size and I had to do a terrific back flip under water to keep from colliding with it. I yelled at the top of my lungs and shot down past the shark, almost catching its fin under my arm. It was as big around as a cow and turned almost on its tail towards me. It was in no way frightened, but was somewhat curious and annoyed and stayed very close to me. I did not want to appear frightened either, so I gradually eased down to the bottom, the shark following quietly. I picked up a piece of dead coral rock about the size of a grapefruit and returned to the surface, being much in need of air. I didn't swim straight up because I wanted to keep my eye on the shark at all times. Instead, I swam up in a long glide with my head turned back toward the shark. When I returned to the surface, I gasped in air for a few minutes and noticed that the shark was practically under my feet. I was really frightened for the tide was rising and this fish appeared to be definitely hunting for food. The giant creature was now circling me at a distance of about eight feet and I waited until it was turning away from me before throwing the rock. In the past, I had frightened away many sharks in this manner. It seems that an object coming from above the surface is so unnatural to them that they will usually flee in terror. But this time it didn't work. The rock missed the shark's back and the splash had no effect on it. It just wouldn't scare! I became quite worried and decided not to do anything foolish. My boat was nearly half a mile away and of course no one was in it so I could not expect any outside help. I began to think that this was my time to go and no one would know what had happened to me. One thing, though, was in my favor: I found that as long as I faced the shark, so that it could see my eyes, it would keep its distance. At least there would be no surprise attack. I didn't have a knife with me because I had lost so many of them in the past that I discontinued carrying them. My only protection was a small hand net and the short piece of rod I used for moving urchins out of the way.

I wondered what I would do if the shark grabbed me. I once saw a shark attack a barracuda under water and it went so fast, that I didn't actually see it grab the fish. I only saw the fish disappear and the shark appear to swallow something. It occurred in shallow water and made a splash of at least a hundred feet which was apparently caused by its tail as it stopped abruptly to keep from running aground. Every fish in the area took cover at the moment of attack and a few minutes later things returned to normal as though nothing had happened. I thought about this as the big fish circled me. I had a superb chance to observe it in detail and couldn't help but marvel at the ease and gracefulness with which it swam through the water. It would glide effortlessly through the water moving only its tail as a rudder to guide it on its course. Its eyes never left me and after about fifteen minutes of endless stalking, I decided that perhaps the shark wasn't going to eat me after all. I began a few experimental dives down to about fifteen feet, keeping the shark in view at all times. Although the big fellow followed me down, it didn't appear to be any more aggressive than before. No doubt it was hungry, but it was cowardly and skeptical and wasn't sure about wanting to attack me. I am sure that if I had panicked and swam blindly towards the boat, it would have grabbed me from behind, for it always seemed to come after my legs.

I decided to stay firm and see if I could eventually unnerve it and drive it away. I swam towards it a few more times, but like before it was in no way frightened of me and I decided not to press the issue. I am not certain what kind of shark it was, but it weighed well in excess of a thousand pounds and it was at least fourteen to sixteen feet long. It had the characteristic bluish color and tail structure of a mako shark and, since I had nearly two hours to observe it, I would say it was either a very large mako or possibly a great white shark.

After about a half hour had passed, it seemed to lose interest in me and swam off about twenty feet or more where it seemed to wait as though meditating. I had been quite unnerved by the whole ordeal, but since I hadn't actually been attacked, and since I was in such a good collecting area, I decided to continue my collecting. In my business if you got out of the water every time you saw a shark, you would never get any collecting done. The sky had clouded up overhead giving the area a very gloomy effect, and each dive I made I had the fear of impending doom. The shark seemed to disappear for a little while, but returned again, this time staying just at the edge of my line of vision. It was incredible how his color matched the sea. If I didn't know he was there, I would never have seen him. As he swam towards me, his body would be clearly outlined, but when he swam past, his features would blend so perfectly with the water that he would become practically invisible, though he was but a short distance away. This was quite frightening for at any minute I would expect him to come dashing out of the gloom and I wouldn't be able to see him until he was practically upon me. I could not concentrate on collecting anymore because I kept turning around under water, trying to keep my eye on the shark, while at the same time trying to locate a specimen. My nerves were shot but the worst was yet to come!

The big shark had been appearing and reappearing for about two hours and was evidently getting impatient. Suddenly, I noticed a quickening in its pace. Its body seemed to quiver and it began circling me very quickly. I knew now that it was going to attack! If I was frightened before, I was terrified now. It would come at me so fast that I wouldn't see it until it was right up against me! It made several lightning passes at me, each time almost breaking the surface, and the turbulance of its powerful body passing so close whirled me about in the water. I was certain it was trying to grab my legs and I had my body crouched into a tight ball with my head under water, trying to face it each time as it reached me. It was a terrifying experience. I decided that since the shark was going to bite me I'd best head for the boat, figuring that if it did bite me, it would probably do it nonchalantly, taking a bite at a time. At least if I got to the boat, I could somehow stop the bleeding and head for shore. I was in a very remote area little traveled by other boats and felt very much alone and insignificant. I swam back to the boat mostly under water and in an erratic fashion so that I could keep my eye on the shark, who was following like a hungry wolf. Several times when it became over-anxious, I had to crouch into a tight ball. The shark just didn't seem to want to attack while I was facing it.

I finally did reach the boat and paused to look around before my last leap to safety. Then I practically flew into the boat. I had expected to feel the shark's teeth in my legs all the way back to the boat and when I finally got aboard, I was so badly frightened that I not only gave up collecting for the day, but very nearly for good. Even to this day, although I still nearly always dive alone, I have a terrible fear of diving in murky water and am always apprehensive when I submerge in the gloomy depths.

The biggest shark I ever saw was the giant whale shark that was captured in the Bahamas. Its total weight was between twenty and thirty thousand pounds and its mouth was nearly six feet wide! The monstrous creature was towed in from the Gulf Stream and photographer Ralph Bowden and myself took underwater movies of it while it was still alive. It was so huge that just to swim from one end of it to the other took considerable effort because there was a strong current that day. I found it easier to crawl rather than swim along the giant creature's body and this worked fine until I discovered that I was bleeding badly. The creature's skin was as rough as sandpaper and it had scraped my flesh bare in many places, which I hadn't noticed because of the excitement. This was very painful and was aggravated by the mucous or slime from the whale's skin. To add to the discomfort, there were numerous sharks cruising a short distance away, but, fortunately, none of them came close, probably because we had several boats anchored in the near vicinity. We took turns swimming around the giant fish to show on film the comparison in size between a human and the monstrous fish and when one of us would swim off towards the gigantic tail, we would appear very tiny, almost like ants climbing on an elephant. We climaxed the movie with a close-up shot of the creature's tremendous mouth, which was opening and closing rhythmically, and I swam up to the giant head and peered into the cavernous maw. I had placed one arm on the lower jaw and held my other arm above me so that I could feel the upper jaw when it came down and then could pull my head out in time. It made a good movie and although I was wearing full aqualung equipment, I could

Giant whale shark (Rhinedon typus) captured in Bimini was towed into shallow water by Capt. John Cass and aroused tremendous interest on the island. The author and Ralph Bowden took underwater movies of the huge creature, which was nearly 40 feet long. (Photo by the author courtesy Lyon, Inc., Bimini, B.W.I.)

easily have swam down inside the creature's gullet with room to spare.

Writing about sharks often stirs the imagination to what could have happened during the actual encounter. When I first prepared a report at the request of Mr. F. G. Wood, Jr., curator of Marine Studios, Florida, I spent considerable time recording my encounters with sharks so that I could make the report as accurate as possible. Writing about sharks makes a diver much more conscious of them, for shortly after I had finished the first phase of the report, I encountered three sharks in a single afternoon. One was a large mako and a dangerous fellow for he was on the prowl for food. I had just finished the report on the big mako that nearly got me, and the whole nerve-wracking experience was still vivid in my mind, when right in front of me was still another large mako. I felt the hair stand up on the back of my neck and little goosepimples rose on my arms. Was this to be another harrowing experience like the last one, I wondered as the big fish circled me. Fortunately, it wasn't, for evidently he was just curious. He swam around me for a few minutes and then vanished as quickly as he had appeared. Later that same month the newspapers reported two shark accounts in local waters. One grabbed a skin diver who had been playing with it, and the fish had such a firm hold on the boy's flesh that its jaws had to be cut out with a knife. The other incident involved a man who was pulled beneath the surface by a shark while clinging to a boat. His body was later discovered with numerous shark bites.

Many people ask where sharks are most likely to be encountered. They may be found anywhere in the sea, from the shallow water to great depths. I have seen large, dangerous sharks very close to shore in water so shallow that they could hardly swim. I have seen them in dirty, brackish, almost fresh water where they certainly would never be expected. In short, it can be said that wherever there is salt water there is likely to be a shark. Of course, sharks are much more plentiful in the deeper water, but the average person is less likely to encounter them there since most people don't swim in the high seas by their own choosing.

Although I have encountered many sharks in my diving career, the above accounts are certainly the exception and not the rule. I have found that small sharks up to six or seven feet will usually scurry away at top speed when they encounter a man. I have also found that large sharks, especially makos, are usually accompanioned by a school of jacks. These smaller fish will swim rapidly around a diver, no doubt pointing him out to the shark who will then swim in and survey the proposed meal. As stated before, it

I swam up to the giant creature and placed my hand firmly on its lower jaw.

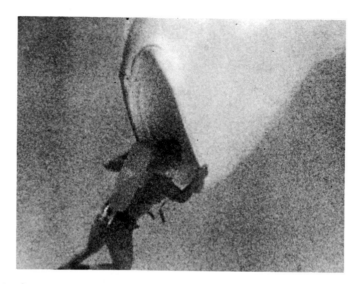

As the 40-foot shark opened its mouth, I peered inside while Ralph ground away with the movie camera. It was a whale shark, the largest fish in the world.

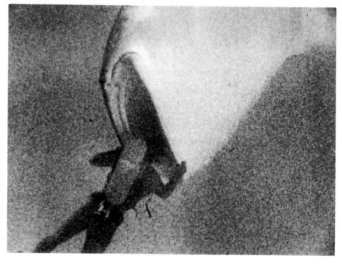

The whale shark doesn't have teeth like regular sharks. Instead of biting you, it inhales you. I held onto both jaws as I looked further inside, and when they began to close, I got the heck out of there fast. (Photos by Ralph Bowden, courtesy Lyon, Inc.)

seems that sharks nearly always approach from behind and will usually swim away as soon as you turn to face them. I once had a graphic example of this when I was photographing some small, colorful fish in eighty feet of water. I felt a slight nudging against my back and ignored it assuming it to be a gorgonian or other sea growth and continued with my work. When I finally turned, I almost stuck my head right into the mouth of an enormous shark. I didn't have time to get a good look at it and I don't remember exactly what I did, but I do know that the shark turned tail and disappeared almost instantly. This seems to be their general behavior making them quite cowardly creatures.

Sharks will usually investigate any splashing or struggling in the water, but often stay at the edge of the diver's vision so that they are unnoticed. Many times underwater I have turned suddenly to see the tail of a shark scurrying quickly away. They come in to investigate and retreat rapidly once discovered. Based upon my own personal experiences, I can say that sharks will usually follow and survey a lone swimmer for some time before attacking him. It would appear that if the swimmer does not panic and swim frantically for the surface, there is much less chance that he will be attacked. This seems to be particularly true in water that is not especially clear. In very clear water, the shark usually observes the diver from some distance away and an attack may be very fast, especially if there is blood or signs of struggling. Anyone who has ever seen how fast a shark can move underwater would realize how futile it is to try to beat the shark back to the boat. If a shark is intent upon attack, I doubt if a swimmer could go more than a few feet before the shark would get him.

My personal opinion about sharks is that they are never to be trusted. Very few are harmless, including the much hunted nurse shark. Large sharks should always be feared. Their size alone makes them dangerous and they aren't likely to be afraid of you if you dive at them and yell. When they are big enough, they just don't scare. They look at you with curiosity, and if they want to eat you they go right ahead. Your best bet is not to bother with the big fellows. If you encounter one, swim quietly towards the boat keeping your eyes on him at all times. Then go aboard quickly, pulling your feet up as fast as possible.

What should the skin diver do when he meets a large shark out on a reef? Is he in danger, or will the shark only molest him if he is bleeding or holding on to a speared fish? There has been a great deal written about sharks and shark behaviour in the past few years. Unfortunately, much of the material was written by people who had never seen a shark in the water. They based their opinions and advice largely on scientific theory, and more often than not completely disregarded most, if not all, information supplied by the skin diver. I have encountered my share of sharks, moray eels, and barracuda in my thirty thousand hours of skin diving, and even as I write this chapter, my hands are a bit shaky from a hair rising encounter with a gigantic tiger shark that happened just a short while ago. I still shudder when I think of that monstrous killer, nearly twenty feet long, who stalked me in the murky water off Miami and who rushed down upon me from out of the gloom. It was a frightening experience and it will be a long time before I forget those bright, bird-like eyes and that tremendous mouth that actually seemed to be smiling with an evil smirk as though the creature anticipated a fine meal.

I was diving by myself and the water was very dirty. I should never have gone under in such conditions, but I thought I would take a chance. It's strange, but I could almost feel the presence of that shark in the water about me. Things were just right for a shark attack. The water was extremely murky with visibility at less than ten feet, and the tide was coming in fast. I had my first warning of impending danger when a huge school of amberjack swam about me at lightning speed as though the very devil was after them. I had learned from past experiences that when a school of amberjack or even a single jack or remora suddenly appears out of the gloom that it's a good indication that a large shark is cruising about looking for a meal. These smaller fish often lead a shark to its meal and feed on the small pieces as the shark tears chunks of flesh off its victim.

I was collecting specimens for aquariums and didn't want to leave so I stayed in the water. I strained my eyes in every direction for the telltale outline of the shark, but the water was so dirty and the incoming tide was moving the debris so quickly through the water that it was impossible to see very much. I shrugged off the scare of the jacks that had visited me so suddenly and went back to work. About fifteen minutes passed and with each minute I felt that I was a fool to stay in the water. I sighted a beautiful Townsend angelfish and proceeded to catch it in my small collecting net. It was difficult to see the fish from the surface so I would take a deep breath and dive to the bottom in my attempt to catch it. Collecting fish with a hand net in this fashion is extremely dangerous because in order to catch the elusive little creatures the diver must concentrate on them completely, not taking his eye off them for even a second. If it's a long dive of a minute or a minute and a half, a lot can happen while the diver is on the bottom. This is a prime situation for an attack by a large green moray eel or a hungry shark due to the diver thrashing his legs to maintain his position, thereby appearing to be struggling or wounded. I had taken extra breaths so I could stay down longer and was concentrating on catching the little fish when a huge dark shape cut out the light above my head. I crouched against the bottom and the tremendous tiger shark swooped down over me in a fast glide. The creature was so big that I couldn't help but stare at it in awe! Then it disappeared into the murky gloom, leaving a cloud of mud where it had almost crashed into the bottom. I knew from past experiences that it had not gone away. I was frightened and expected a second attack any second. Tiger sharks usually watch their victim for fifteen or twenty minutes before they finally engulf it, and I quickly realized that the time was up and I had better get out of there fast. But rather than swim madly back to the boat, which I knew might further provoke an attack, I swam at a medium pace, watching behind me as well as ahead all the while. When I got to the boat, I jumped aboard and shook for a few minutes. I hope I have sense enough not to dive again in dirty water, especially alone.

The above encounter might prove helpful to skin divers who have an encounter with a large shark. The event is likely to be nerve-wracking, particularly if the diver is alone. I can say from experience that an encounter with a large shark or green moray eel is far more frightening when the diver is all alone with no one in the boat for consolation. It's true that most sharks won't bother swimmers, but it's the ones that do bother them that cause concern. No one can say that a shark will *positively* not attack a diver if he does not molest it. A more accurate statement would be that sharks *usually* will not bother a diver if he doesn't molest it. People often ask me if I am afraid of sharks. I answer, "Only when I am in the water with them." No one can predict the behaviour of a large shark.

I always specify large sharks in my writings on these creatures, as small sharks are not likely to be dangerous. They are usually very easy to frighten and even if they do attack, the wound is not likely to be serious and the diver can easily cope with them. Small sharks are sharks under three or four feet. Any shark larger than this is a potential danger. Large sharks, ten to twenty feet or over, can be extremely dangerous, ESPECIALLY IF THE WATER IS DIRTY. This is one cardinal rule I would like to pass on to skin divers. Never spear fish in dirty water and NEVER DIVE ALONE. I dive alone out of necessity, but I never go alone if I can take someone with me, and after my last hair-raising experience, I doubt that I will ever dive alone again in dirty water. I have had too many close shaves.

If you meet a shark out on the reef, don't panic. Just stay there and face him. Chances are he will look you over and swim away. But don't count on him to stay away. If you are spearing fish and he hears the thrashing of the fish or smells blood in the water, he will return. Usually, his first approach will be very cautious, but if he is hungry he will become bolder. When you spear your next fish, you might find him right on your shoulder, waiting to eat the fish. If he acts too aggressive it would be wise to return to the boat, but if you are accompanied by several divers and the water is calm and clear, you may be able to frighten the shark away so that you won't have to give up your diving area. If the water is murky, it would be wise to move to another spot rather than take a chance.

One of the most frightening ways to meet a shark is in shallow inshore water in the Florida Keys where the big hammerheads cruise looking for food. It is quite disturbing to surface for a breath of air and see a huge black fin cutting through the water heading right toward you. This is how a hammerhead swims in the shallows and often he will cruise for long periods with his dorsal and tip of his tail breaking the water. Sometimes the fin will be bone dry on a calm day. When a hammerhead approaches you in this manner, you have no alternative but to submerge and face him under water, for if you left your legs dangling down from the surface, there is a good chance he will grab them. Hammerheads grow to good size and twelve- to fifteen-foot monster is not uncommon even in very shallow water. I have seen fifteen-foot specimens in water so shallow that part of their back was out of it. They cruise the shallows for sting rays and eagle rays, which are two of their favorite foods next to tarpon and skin divers. They are one of the most common sharks found in shallow water so that divers working near shore will certainly encounter them when the water is reasonably warm.

In fact, sharks are fairly common in Florida and Bahama waters during certain times of the year. Sometimes they are all over and you may see schools of them out near the Gulf Stream. At other times they are scarce and you may not encounter one for months. They are usually more common in the spring and summer, but you can never be certain at any time that a huge shark won't suddenly come out of the gloom and head for you at top speed. More often than not sharks swim in and investigate skin divers or circle around entirely unobserved. This is because sharks usually approach from behind and because their color changes to match the color of the water conditions. I have seen huge sharks cruising around me just at the periphery of my vision so that it was almost impossible to see them. They would appear as a ghost image barely discernible as they cruised silently about.

Sharks don't stand out except in extremely clear water or in shallow water above white sand. They usually blend their colors with the surroundings so that they are as inconspicuous as possible. We once caught a hammerhead shark that was bright orange. It had been swimming beneath a huge patch of sargassum weed out in the Gulf Stream and was caught by a friend on a spinning rod. We couldn't figure out what it was with its strange orange color. Imagine our surprise when we saw that it was an orange shark!

The sharks that you don't see are the ones that are the most dangerous. Some sharks attack at top speed when they are in a feeding mood. This is why it is so dangerous to skin dive and especially to spearfish in water that is not clear. When a shark sights his food, he knows he must grab it fast before it gets away, and in dirty water a shark is likely to grab a diver's arm or leg as it flashes in the water, thinking it is a fish. He may not see the whole diver when he begins his attack since he is often led to the area by the vibrations of the diver or the thrashing about of a speared fish. Blood in the water also attracts sharks and excites them to feeding. If the water is clear, the shark will have plenty of time to see the whole diver and will usually swerve away before he has approached too closely. Also, the diver will be able to see the shark and turn to face it, which will usually discourage an attack since sharks are cowards and nearly always attack from behind. I feel that facing a shark when he approaches the diver is the best safeguard against attack. If you show no fear and are even a little aggressive, you can usually unnerve a shark and eventually drive him away. But don't count on hollering, blowing bubbles, and threatening gestures to frighten away a big shark. Some sharks just don't scare, especially the big fellows. They might turn on you to defend themselves and if they do, you are in trouble. A shark can swim circles around the best skin diver. If you have ever seen a shark swim at top speed, you will see the futility of trying

Contrary to popular belief, sharks are very common in Florida and Bahama waters. Here natives hold the giant head of a large ground shark harpooned in the shallow waters around Bimini. (Photo by the author courtesy Lyon, Inc., Bimini, B.W.I.)

to beat him to the boat. The safest rule to follow regarding sharks is that if the shark is very large, from twelve to twenty feet, you should gradually work your way to the boat, keeping the shark in view at all times. If he rushes you, turn and face him until he has turned away and then swim to the boat still keeping him in view. Should he come very close, you have no alternative but to hit him in the face with a spear or pipe. No diver should enter the water without either a spear, gig, or a short piece of pipe for protection. I have lost track of the number of large green morays, barracuda, and sharks that I have had to tap on the nose with a piece of pipe to discourage aggressive behaviour on their part.

I suspect that the shark picture would be clarified considerably if all the attacks around the world were accurately reported. I know of several attacks in this area that were suppressed from the news possibly because of the adverse effect on the tourist trade, and I am sure that there are many attacks south of the border in Central and South America that are not recorded. I think that if the actual figures could be obtained, the annual shark attack around the world would be five to ten times what it is reported to be today. I don't believe that sharks attack people only because they mistake them for a fish, or that sharks won't ever attack you if you don't molest them. The fact that millions of bathers use the beaches every year and only a few are attacked by sharks on both coasts every year doesn't necessarily mean that sharks aren't a real danger. Consider first that sharks are cowardly. There is so much commotion on a public beach that sharks stay off shore rather than swim in with all the people. Also there are life guards on hand who get the people out of the water when sharks are sighted. This has probably prevented many attacks. In addition, the

Those who feel that shark attacks are rare or only happen to Australian bathers should take interest in these clippings from the Miami *Herald*.

sharks that will attack people are in the minority so that the over-all chance of a person being attacked by sharks is minimal. A skin diver, however, has a much better chance of becoming shark liver because he is isolated from the masses of people that might ordinarily frighten the creatures. He also invades deeper water than the bather and if he is spearing fish he attracts sharks and stirs them into a feeding mood. It's a wonder more divers aren't attacked. Many do have close calls where a shark grabs their flipper or takes a fish from their hands but we are fortunate more divers are not molested. It must be that skin divers are so alert and aware of the fact that sharks do present a danger that they automatically take precautions. But sharks are still a problem and the diver can greatly reduce his chances of being attacked by diving in clear water, diving with one or more persons, and by keeping a watchful eye for sharks, especially at the extreme edge of visibility. Look closely next time you dive. You just might see the ghostly outline of a great white shark or hammerhead that has been swimming silently around you for the past half hour. Remember it's the shark you don't see that will cause the most trouble. You can bet your snorkle he'll see you.

5
The Floating Death!

THE MOST HORRIBLE EXPERIENCE OF MY LIFE HAPPENED down in the Florida Keys on what started out to be a perfect day. I was violating the number one diver's rule: I was diving alone. The sky was beautifully clear and the ocean was flat with a faint westerly breeze that picked up ever so slightly as I headed out to sea.

Although the seas were calm, the water was very dirty, which is usually the case when the wind comes from the west, stirring up the white marl on the coastal flats and carrying it seaward. Murky water is the bane of the skin diver for it allows sharks, barracuda, and other predators to swim in close to the diver and remain undetected. I thought about this as I looked for a suitable reef to work. Lately there had been many sharks in the water, and just a few days before I had encountered two huge fourteen-foot hammerhead sharks. I don't normally dive in dirty water, but on this day I thought I would chance it as I had done many times in the past. I prayed that I wouldn't meet any sharks. Little did I realize that I would run into something far worse and that it would almost take my life.

I had anchored over a small reef and had collected a number of colorful fish including the dainty butterfly fish, clown wrasse, angelfish, porcupine fish, and several other varieties for which I had orders, but the water was so dirty that I decided to move to another location. The wind had increased in intensity and was blowing straight from shore. As a rule, the west wind is the worst for skindiving as it is unpredictable and invariably brings trouble. Somehow I had a premonition of disaster as I dove that day.

I soon located another small reef abundant with choice fish, and in a short while had caught a good quantity of them. I was elated with my success and had just returned to the surface with a net full of fish when tragedy struck. As I turned around in the water to place the fish in my floating collecting basket, I felt the sickening shock from contact with a man-of-war. The man-of-war seemed to envelop me with a series of quick electric jolts. I had been stung several times before, but I instantly knew that this was a very bad encounter, since I was completely enveloped by the tendrils of this deadly creature. I dropped everything and quickly turned and swam back to the boat, which fortunately was only a few hundred feet away. I staggered frantically aboard and saw the evil, glistening body of the dreadful creature clinging to my back. The pain was already unbearable and I grabbed the evil mass with my bare hands and tore it from my neck and shoulders. By now my back was completely paralyzed. I knew then that I was in real danger for usually when pain leaves the body during a serious accident it's because the nerves are deadened and no longer transmit the pain signals. I could feel a terrible tightening of my muscles and a creeping sensation of paralysis gradually moving over my entire body.

The deadly tentacles were still fastened tightly to my back and underarms and I realized that I had made a 100 per cent contact with the horrible creature and that all its

The deadly man-of-war jellyfish (Physalia) with its thousands of poisonous stinging cells hanging in coils beneath it is probably more of a menace to swimmers and divers in the Bahamas and Florida than sharks and other dangerous fish. It can inflict torturous pain that may hospitalize or render the victim unconscious.

poisonous, stinging tentacles had struck me at one time. I began to feel dizzy and nauseated and began stripping off the blue strings of poison. They adhered so tightly to my flesh that I could not get them loose, so I began digging them off with the sharp end of my knife. I somehow removed all the tentacles from my neck, arms, and legs, but could not reach a huge cluster that was firmly imbedded on my shoulder and back. I looked back helplessly at the quivering, deadly mass clinging there, vibrating and pulsating as it injected poison from its thousands of stinging cells and I was in utter despair for I just could not reach them. They were fastened so tightly that they became fused to the swollen flesh. In desperation, I looked about me and noticed a small boat about a mile and a half away and decided to go to it for help. I frantically pulled up the anchor and started the motor. There was an air leak in the gas tank hose and it had been giving me a little trouble but I had ignored it as I intended to have it repaired in the near future. Now, it really gave trouble! I was in such intense pain and in a wild state of delirium, that I cranked the motor over and over again. It sputtered and coughed and would quit after I had gone only a few feet.

I thought for certain I was finished as I fought consciousness for now I couldn't even go for help. I waved a piece of white cloth, but of course no one could see it and I tried the motor once more. Finally it caught and I headed grimly for the distant boat. By now my anguish was at a peak and I slapped myself repeatedly to keep from losing consciousness. I had but one thought in mind and that was survival. I had to reach that boat and have someone remove the clinging death from my burning shoulders. I drove the boat at top speed and was in a state of near panic. My mind was fogged and I clutched the knife tightly in one hand, repeating over and over aloud, "the tentacles must be cut off, the tentacles must be cut off." As I approached the boat, I saw that it was occupied by a skindiver who stood up as I drew near. He looked as though he had seen a ghost! I must have looked like a madman to him, for I headed straight at him, standing up in the boat with arm extended, grimly holding the knife. My eyes were glazed and my teeth clenched, my mouth was covered with foamy saliva. I think he feared I was going attack him. As I approached closer, I slowed down and pulled along side.

"Help me, help me!" was all I could utter.

"What's your trouble?" he asked, bewildered.

Without answering, I turned around and showed him the bluish mass of tentacles and he quickly understood.

"Cut them off for me, will you," I begged, as I handed him the knife.

"Just a second and I'll get a rag," he said. He grabbed a piece of cloth from the bow and stripped off the clusters of stinging pain from my shoulders, which by now were completely without feeling.

Then I began to scream and jump around in the boat, as the full effect of the deadly poison took hold.

The dumbfounded diver was at a loss of what to do. He finally rubbed a bottle of sun-tan lotion over the burning area and said he was sorry but that was all he knew to do about the severe stinging.

I threw myself to the bottom of the boat, twisting and squirming as I went into a state of near shock. My body began to go rigid and soon I had extreme difficulty in breathing.

I began screaming, "It's killing me! It's killing me! I'm dying!"

The diver looked on in amazement. He summoned his buddy from the water and the two of them watched help-

Dainty blue and black nomeus swim in among the deadly tentacles of the man-of-war and live a precarious existence by retreating into the tentacles for safety and luring larger fish to their death.

lessly from their boat which one of them had tied to mine. Apparently both felt there was nothing they could do.

As the full effect of the poison hit me, I felt more pain than I had ever felt before in my life. In the past I had suffered from kidney pains, which are indeed horrible, and doctors at the hospital had informed me that they are probably the most acute pains the human body could ever suffer, including childbirth, but they were wrong. These pains were a thousand times more painful. They made my kidney pains feel like a dull toothache by comparison.

I began making loud moans, all the while screaming that I was dying and I am sure I nearly frightened the two skin divers to death. The pain began to creep over my body. My chest tightened up as though an invisible force was squeezing me to death and my lungs no longer would function. I could no longer breathe! My lungs had become paralyzed! I began to suck in air in tiny gasps and I felt that death was near. At first I was frightened, but then I looked forward to it as welcome relief. It would be like going to sleep, I thought. My breathing became even more difficult and I felt I would suffocate. I didn't want to die. I stood up and tried to ask one of the divers to give me artificial respiration but couldn't talk. I made a few unintelligible noises and dropped back to the bottom of the boat. Then I decided that in spite of the pain I must lie still so that I would not need as much air. I reasoned that the poison would work on me more slowly if I stood still. I lapsed in and out of consciousness. As I lay in the boat, the men became very concerned and decided they should get me to a hospital.

"Where did you come from?" one of them asked.

I summoned all of my strength and blurted out, "Garden Cove."

My throat was paralyzed and it was all I could say. I

could see the name meant nothing to them as they were probably tourists on vacation.

"We'll get you to shore," one of them said.

I must have passed out, for the next thing I knew, one of the fellows was in my boat and we were heading towards shore. The other fellow was following behind in their boat. We went for about five minutes, when I suddenly got up from the bottom and told the men that I thought I could make it back by myself. I could breathe again, not normally, but at least I could draw in air.

They asked if I was sure and I said yes. I told them that the crisis was over and that I could breathe fairly well now. I thanked them and apologized for interrupting their skin diving and headed for shore.

Since I nearly always dive alone, I make it a hard, fast rule that if I go out by myself, I will come back in by myself with no assistance. I once rowed a heavy boat eighteen miles when the motor quit on me, rather than be towed in by a passing boat. Only if I was mortally wounded or in danger of sinking, or if a boat was going my way, would I ever accept help.

The temptation was great to let one of the men drive me to shore, but I reasoned that it would take at least two hours since we were heading directly into a heavy, choppy sea with the wind coming straight from shore. I had been stung by many marine organisms before including these same jellyfish, stinging coral, poison coral, scorpion fish, etc., and I knew that eventually the pain would subside and that it would probably be gone by the time we reached shore. It would have ruined the day for both the divers, so I decided to go in alone! I sat up and began to operate the boat.

I slowed the boat momentarily while the skin diver got back on his own boat and after assuring them that I could make it, I grimly headed for shore. They went away in the opposite direction and I watched them slowly disappear from view. I was all alone. I had to make it in now by myself. On the distant shore I could see the high tension

Stinging cells of the man-of-war jellyfish quickly paralyze an unwary fish. The sail of the man-of-war has been pulled down during the fight with the fish.

towers that marked the way home. At this distance they were the only landmarks visible and I headed towards them. It took all my strength to keep the boat headed in the right direction, and the pain in my kidneys and the small of my back was absolutely maddening. I would run the boat for about five minutes and then when I could

My laboratory on Key Largo after it was ravaged by a hurricane.
Months of hard work were destroyed in a day.

stand it no longer, I would fling myself to the deck, which
was now sloshing with water. I was in such pain that I
would just lie there for five or ten minutes at a time, letting the boat go where it would. I finally realized that I
must get up, so with extreme effort I would lift my pain-
racked body back onto the seat and once more head the
boat towards shore. Then, after about five minutes of
gruelling pain, I would slow the engine down again and

throw myself to the bottom of the boat. It seemed to give me relief to lie down. I repeated this procedure over and over again. The boat would turn in crazy circles with no one to steer it, and I scanned the horizon in vain for another boat that might be able to tow me in. Unfortunately, there were none. I usually dive in a remote area and the lone skin diver's boat I had gone to for help was one of the few boats I had seen that day. Although the area is notorious for being nearly depleted of fish by skin divers, and these two divers were the first and only skin divers I had seen in the past two years, a few fanatics constantly maintain the area is alive with skin divers and spear-fishermen. I would have liked to have seen a few of them at this time. I thought how wise the two fellows were to be diving in pairs using the buddy system instead of diving alone like I had been foolishly doing for so many years. Then as I lay in the boat rolling with the sea, I felt myself going to sleep and I knew I had to get up and take command once more. With extreme effort I would slowly pull my body onto the seat. I tried to stand up, thinking it would help restore normal circulation to my body, but I was too weak and my legs would keep on collapsing beneath me.

My only thoughts now were to reach shore where I had a combination fishing camp, marine laboratory, and field headquarters, and I thought how wonderful it would be to get back and lie down on a bed. It seemed like the most wonderful thing in the world. I just pictured it in my mind and wondered if I would ever get there. The seas were very rough and in my state of anguish I ploughed through them at top speed, taking no heed of the waves splashing over the bow. After an hour or so, the water began to creep up over the floorboards and soon there was a definite possibility of the boat becoming swamped. I couldn't have cared less I was in such pain. The waves splashing over the bow seemed to revive me as they crashed into my face and my one thought was to make it to shore as fast as possible. I thought about pulling the plug at the rear of the boat and letting the water out, but I was far too weak to reach over the side and I figured that if I went unconscious, the boat would sink and I would never be found.

Once more I lay down on the deck now completely awash with water. I stretched out fully and pushed my legs under the back seat and lay still. My breathing had returned to normal, and suddenly the deep, intense, gnawing pain in the small of my back completely disappeared. I rested for about ten more minutes and then sat up and headed for shore. All the unbearable pains were gone and I began to get back feeling in my arms and shoulders. Soon the hot burning stings on my back, neck, and underarms became apparent and I knew that the major pain was over. There would now be pain, but at least it would be tolerable. I cut the motor slightly to avoid taking in any more water and set a course for shore. When I reached the docks, I was singing, I was so happy to be alive. My arms and shoulders ached terribly like a first degree burn. I tied up the boat and went into my building where I took a quick shower. I still had hot burning pains and was extremely nervous. I made a quick cup of coffee, gulped it down, and then flung myself down on the bed for a much needed rest. The pain became less intense until finally it settled down to a deep, pulsing pain that penetrated to the bone. It felt as though I had been struck hard across the shoulders with a 2″ x 4″ board. I rested for a couple of hours, and then went to get more specimens that I needed, which I could get near shore without going back into the water. Afterwards I drove the eighty miles home.

When I got home, I examined my back in a mirror and

it was a frightening sight. It looked as though someone had plastered a huge blue and red cobweb over my back. I must have received thousands of stings. My hands ached badly from where I had handled the tentacles in my haste to remove them from my body, and I slept little that night. The next day I again inspected the damaged area and found it was very extensive. I had burns on my hands, under my arms, on my neck, and on one portion of my back there was a solid mass of burns, fourteen inches in diameter! I also had burns on my legs and side.

A few days later I inquired among some acquaintances about their own experiences with the man-of-war jellyfish. Much to my surprise, I found that my experience was not at all unique! One ardent skin diver and marine artist, Russ Smiley, told of his own attack by the dreaded creature. He said it was the most horrible pain he had suffered in his life and that he was in bed for three days! Russ said that some years ago he had been accidentaly shot in the head and neck at close range with a 12 gauge shotgun while on a hunting trip, and although it was very painful it was nothing compared to the man-of-war sting. Also, Capt. Bill Gray, well known marine collector for Miami's fabulous Seaquarium, told me recently that he knows how deadly the man-of-war is. He said that he saw a fellow walk into the Seaquarium from a nearby beach with a large man-of-war on his back, and the fellow was in such extreme pain and shock that they thought for certain he would be dead before they could get him in an abulance to the hospital! Another friend, Rick Fried, was stung on the leg by one and still bears the scar after six years. He had to be towed to shore by his companion since he couldn't even move his leg. Bill Humm, a marine collector in the Miami area, told me of a dead body pulled from the bay covered with the unmistakeable burns from a man-of-war, which

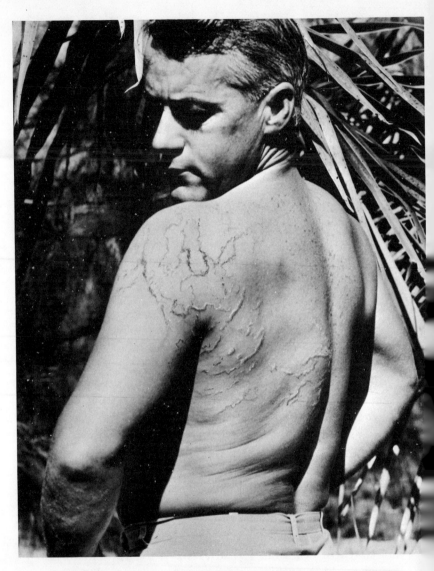

Hideous scars mark the time the author suffered a 100 per cent contact with a large man-of-war jellyfish while diving alone sixteen miles from shore. It was a near fatal encounter, and the author suffered the most diabolical, maddening pain for five hours. The encounter caused temporary unconsciousness, convulsions, and paralysis. (Photo courtesy Rosemary Straughan)

undoubtedly had caused his death. My friend Warren
Prince was stung severely by the man-of-war and was
pulled unconscious from the water. These are just a few
cases among a few acquaintances.

I can sum up the reasons for this near fatal encounter so
that perhaps it may be of help to other divers or swimmers.
First, I was diving in dirty water and could not see properly, otherwise I would have seen the man-of-war before it
had approached too closely and could have swum around
it. Second, the reason this attack was so deadly and nearly
fatal is that I got the full charge of the jellyfish at one time.
Its tentacles were only a few feet long and when it hit me,
I was stung by dozens of tentacles at once, all compressed
together.

Ordinarily, when a swimmer or diver encounters a man-
of-war, the creature has its tentacles extended out ten or
twenty feet and the swimmer encounters only single
strands. These are bad enough, but they usually only result
in bad burns and in no serious poisoning like I received. I
had encountered men-of-war before and been stung quite
badly, but I only received singular burns since the tentacles were distended. I was even able to continue diving
after resting an hour or so. Also, I believe the temperature
of the water has something to do with the intensity of the
burns. It would seem that in very cold water, perhaps because a person's pores are closed, the sting seems to be far
less devastating than in warm water. At any rate, there is
little doubt that when the man-of-war's tentacles are close
drawn to a length of two or three feet, it is the most
deadly, for when its stinging cells are closely concentrated,
it can give its maximum stinging power to a human.

One ironic thing about my attack was that just a week
ago I had read in the newspaper that fifty or more bathers
had been stung by a man-of-war jellyfish, and that many of

them had been rendered unconscious and some required hospitalization. I more or less scoffed at this and reasoned that those who were hospitalized must have been physically weak. Now, I realize how wrong I was. While there is no doubt that the general health of a person is of consequence with respect to the seriousness of a man-o-war sting, the prime factor is the amount of contact with the creature. I am certain that the ordeal I went through would have killed a person in poor physical condition since there are cases of death by man-o-war sting. In my own case, if I had not been close to the boat I would never have made it. Just a half hour earlier, I had been swimming a good half mile from the boat. If I had run into the man-o-war then, I would still be out there.

What can the skin diver or bather do to protect himself against this deadly jellyfish? First of all, he should wear a long sleeved undershirt, preferably in a dark color, and if men-of-war are about, he should scan the immediate area for them before entering the water. He should also never dive alone! It is also wise to carry medication in case of stings. There are some types of ointments said to give immediate relief to the stings. Ammonia and certain soap combinations are also said to offer relief, although I doubt that in a serious case they would be effective. From my own personal experience, I would suggest that if nothing else is available the patient should lie as still as possible so that the poison will flow slowly through the body. In addition, I think that if ice is available it would probably be helpful if applied directly to the wounded area to slow down the poison. Alcohol, gasoline, or other solvents sometimes give relief if applied promptly to the affected area. The best protection, however, is to stay out of the water when they are present. If you ever go through the horrible ordeal, you will never forget it. You will wonder why the good Lord ever created such a hideous creature.

6
Green Morays and Barracuda

CONTRARY TO POPULAR BELIEF, MORAY EELS ARE A POTEN-
tial danger to the skin diver. The reefs are literally full of
moray eels, yet the average swimmer seldom sees them. In
my collecting business it is necessary to peer into caves,
lift up flat rocks, and probe into ledges, and I encounter
dozens and sometimes even hundreds of moray eels nearly
every time I go diving. Although they usually stay in their
homes, some of them are aggressive, and unless you approach them with plenty of warning so that they can see
you well in advance, you may suffer a bad bite or even be
held down until you drown, if grabbed by a large one.

I shall never forget my first encounter with a giant green
moray eel. I was collecting fish on a shallow reef in about
ten feet of water and was making a good haul. I had some
beautiful butterfly fish, black and queen angelfish, neon
gobies, and a scattering of the other colorful fish and
looked forward to a good day, since I was on a reef rich in
marine life. My face mask had become fogged and I decided to clean it. Since the water was very shallow, I simply
placed my net and gloves on the bottom and treaded water

Huge Green Moray peers out at the author from a cave.

while I removed my mask to clean it. I was rinsing the
mask and was about to put it back on when, I noticed a
tremendous dark shape directly beneath me. I wasn't too
alarmed and assumed it to be either a giant barracuda or
a shark. I quickly put on my mask and snorkle to look
beneath the surface. What a shock I had! It was a monstrous green moray eel at least seven or eight feet long! I
was terrified, for I had left my gloves, net, and poker* on

* The poker is a metal pipe used in collecting to move urchins
out of the way or chase the specimen into the net.

the sea floor and the boat was a considerable distance away. I tried to swim sideways without letting my feet down and somehow managed to do a quick jackknife to the bottom, scooping up my net and gloves in one sweeping motion. As I turned, the ugly creature was already upon me with its mouth wide open displaying a jagged row of black teeth that looked like poison daggers. The fierce monster was a foot in diameter and resembled a huge sea serpent. I instinctively pushed my net into its face and I could hear the teeth gnash loudly on the steel frame. It bit savagely into the plastic screen material and nearly wrenched the net from my hands. I pushed and jabbed the net back and forth, trying to knock its teeth out and it soon let go and made a lightning turn under water and, before I knew it, the brute was right up against my thigh, ready to sink its teeth into my stomach. I doubled up under water and again shoved the net into its face. The teeth crunched loudly and I repeated the same procedure as before. The moray did also and moved so fast that I didn't see him until he was coming straight at my face. I held up the net again jabbing viciously, but this time I didn't let the moray bite it. Instead, I repeatedly struck the eel on the end of the nose, moving the net so fast that the moray didn't have time to sink his teeth into it. This new strategy seemed to puzzle the moray and to my relief he swam to the bottom. His mouth was bleeding where I had loosened a few teeth, but he had no intentions of going away. He merely waited to make a new assault. This was my first encounter with a large moray eel and I began to wonder who was going to win. I kept thinking about the misconstrued statements of marine authorities who claimed that the moray looks more vicious than he is and that he would never bother a diver unless he is first molested. I was annoyed that people would make such statements when they really didn't know what they were talking about. I hadn't bothered this fellow in any manner and here he was threatening to eat me alive.

The big moray coiled up directly under my feet and suddenly shot straight at me as though fired from a gun. I was fighting for my life now, for if he ever got a hold of me he would drown me for certain or, at the least, badly mangle me. I jabbed and pushed with the net, which by now had been torn to shreds, and again the moray settled to the bottom. He made several dozen more attacks at me and I wondered if he would ever give up. I was getting very tired and cold since it was winter and I hadn't donned my rubber diving suit. I had learned when to expect his sudden attacks by the undulation of his coils. I began to get impatient and started to swim down to meet the attacks. This worked better, for he wouldn't have time to coil his body properly for his lightning dart through the water. I hit and banged his head hundreds of times yet he wouldn't go away. Finally in exasperation I decided to rush him, and I dove down upon him intending to unnerve him and frighten him away, but he was absolutely fearless. He just stayed there and waited for me and opened his mouth wider than I ever thought he could. It was opened absolutely straight up and down like a rattlesnake about to strike. He turned to face me as if to engulf me in one huge swallow and I stayed my distance. This big fellow just would not scare. If I had gone any closer he positively would have grabbed me. I retreated to the surface and he didn't follow, but stayed in the exact spot, his mouth still wide open. I took advantage of his temporary stupor and quickly swam to my innertube, which was anchored a few hundred feet away. I quietly loosened the small anchor line and swam back towards the boat, which was anchored at the other end of the reef. I kept glancing in back of me but the moray apparently had enough, for he didn't follow. I climbed back into the boat and rested a long while and reviewed the incident over and over in my mind. I was angry with all the experts on marine life who had stated in their books and literature that morays will seldom if ever bother a skindiver, and I decided that probably most of them had done little or no skindiving and were merely repeating the statements of other "experts," who probably spent most of their time at a desk or in a library reading about such things rather than actually experiencing them.

I stayed in the boat for several hours to warm up and rest, but mainly to get courage to go back into the water. I should have had more sense than to go back in right on the same reef, but it had been such a good collecting area that I hated to leave it. I decided I would stay near the boat at the end of the reef, which was at least a thousand feet from where I had encountered the giant moray. I got another net and went back into the water. The collecting wasn't as good at this end of the reef as it was on the other side, but I managed to catch some fish nonetheless. No doubt I was so nervous trying to look in all directions at once that I couldn't concentrate properly. Also, the sun had disappeared behind heavy clouds, making the water very gloomy, which didn't help my feelings, for visibility was vastly impaired. I was chasing a blue angelfish around a large head of coral when I paused momentarily to look in back of me. There was the big green moray all coiled and ready to strike. I was so disgusted and angry that I didn't even give him a second look. I let the angelfish go and swam back to the boat, which luckily was close by, and leaped aboard expecting any second to feel the cruel teeth of the moray sink into my legs. I started the motor, hauled in my innertube, and headed for home. I just didn't feel like giving that gigantic green moray another chance to get me.

Even to this day, although I know exactly where the reef is located, I have never visited it again, so vividly can I recall that harrowing undersea battle. When I think back about it now I wonder just why the huge creature attacked me. The only logical reasons I can offer is that either it had a nest nearby or it merely assumed ownership of the reef and drove intruders away. I am certain that the second time the creature appeared at the opposite end of the reef, it had been attracted by my metal poker hitting against the coral. It no doubt associated me with that noise and came to investigate.

This wasn't the only time I have been menaced by moray eels. Although it was the most prolonged attack, it was not the most brazen. Another time when I encountered the monster eel, I was in about thirty feet of water and swimming along the surface bothering no one. I came to a tremendous lump coral formation that was as large as a house and decided to explore it. I swam around it, marveling at its beauty when I noticed a large cave emerging from one end. I decided to explore this, so I took a deep breath and quietly submerged.

I have always made it a practice to approach caves from the top and with great caution so that if there is a large jewfish living there, I will be able to see it before it sees me and thereby probably save myself from being swallowed whole. I used the same procedure this time, and when I reached the cave, I placed my hands on the upper rim and quietly eased my head over the edge so that I could see inside. The cave was huge, and arched over a long flat ledge. It took my eyes a few moments to become accustomed to the semi-darkness, but when I finally could see, I stared in awe at a truly gigantic green moray eel! It was

Green morays are utterly fearless and on occasion will attack a diver without any provocation. The author has had several attack him. In one instance a giant eight-foot-long monster attacked, swimming all the way from the bottom in thirty-five feet of water to do battle on the surface.   (Photo courtesy Marineland of Florida)

stretched out full length and I would say it was at least eight feet long! It was stretched out perfectly straight and its body was puffed up with water or air so that it looked to be fifteen or eighteen inches in diameter. I pushed my head away from the opening and without a ripple I floated back to the surface. I started to swim away and figured that the giant eel hadn't seen me. I was approximately fifty feet from the huge coral head and was about to give a sigh of relief when I noticed the big green head of the eel poke out of a hole in the coral. I started to swim rapidly away, assuming that if I put enough distance between me and the coral, the eel would stay there since I hadn't molested it, but I was wrong. When I turned again in the direction of the coral, I noticed that the giant eel had left the coral and was right at the surface some thirty feet above. It was swimming very slowly. I was now about eighty feet away and still saw no reason why the eel would bother me. I thought perhaps it wasn't interested in me at all, so I changed directions to see if the eel would follow. It did! I guess it decided I was getting away because suddenly it quickened its pace and soon was right next to me. Its mouth was closed, and as it got closer I wondered just what it wanted. I didn't have to wait long to find out, for it soon arched its head, made a loop of its body, and jabbed straight at me with its mouth wide-open. Again, my only protection was my plastic screened hand net, and I jabbed this in its face, twisting and turning it so that it couldn't get a good bite at it. We tumbled and rolled through the water and once or twice I felt the slimy body slap against my bare skin. It was a miracle that I wasn't bitten—the eel could move so much faster than me under water—but when the foam and bubbles of our struggle cleared away, I couldn't find any injuries. This eel wasn't as game as the last one, even though it was considerably larger. Perhaps it was due to the water being so deep, for no doubt eels feel uncomfortable when they are too far away from the protective coral. At any rate, this eel didn't put up much of a fight. After the first encounter it darted swiftly down into the coral. I took advantage of this and decided to be the aggressor so that when the eel made a second attempt to attack, I met it halfway up from the bottom and beat it savagely on the head with my net. This proved too much for it and it retreated for good. I didn't want any surprise encounters with it, so I swam back to the boat and went to another reef.

I have found in my years of diving and collecting that moray eels are truly dangerous creatures. While it is generally true that moray eels don't go out looking for trouble, I can say that some of them definitely do and I have had at least thirty of them menace me dangerously, and if I had ignored them, they would have attacked me.

It is only the large morays, five feet or over, that are really dangerous. These creatures have powerful jaws and if one clamps on to your arm or leg, it may either drown you or tear such a huge chunk of flesh from your body that you will bleed to death. When a large moray grabs its victim, it will inflate its body so that it can't be dislodged from the coral. Then it will spin its body around and around until its victim is terribly mangled.

I have had so many close shaves with the big green morays that I sometimes think I am living on borrowed time. I once had one grab me in the side and all it got was a mouth full of rubber from my rubber suit. Luckily, I had been wearing heavy woolen underwear beneath the suit and this had saved my skin. I didn't even see the moray until I felt the cold water rushing into my suit and turned to see the big green head still holding the mouthful of black rubber in its jaws. I had been working in among a huge jumble of brain coral, and the eel had made a quick grab at my body as it passed by an opening in the coral.

Although morays are quite fearless when they get over five feet, the smaller specimens are not so brave, and I usually make it a practice to tap them on the nose with my poker as soon as they poke their heads out at me so that they won't get any bright ideas. This usually teaches them that you won't take any nonsense from them, and they retract their heads and usually give no further trouble.

I can almost guarantee that if you stick your hand suddenly into a hole containing a moray eel, he will instinctively bite you, either for his own protection or out of anger. Many times I have pushed my poker into a dark ledge and felt the metallic click as a moray grabbed it. One time in particular, I had spotted an especially beautiful hermit crab walking along the bottom. As I approached, it darted into a small, dark hole. I removed my glove and was just about to reach two fingers into the narrow opening when my better judgment told me I should use my poker to get the hermit crab out of the hole. I stuck the poker in the opening to get the crab and a powerful set of jaws clamped down on it immediately. Probably the crab had attracted the moray to the opening, but I am certain that if my fingers had gone down there instead of the poker I would have a most difficult time typing today. It just doesn't pay to take chances under the sea.

Small morays, of course don't have to be feared much, because the worse they can do is bite off a finger or two. I have become so accustomed to handling them that I catch them in a shallow hand net and sometimes throw them in the boat until I come aboard and can put them in a covered container. Although they seem sluggish under a rock, they can swim like lightning when they are forced out in the open. Also, they are difficult to keep in the net once they are aroused. They will shoot straight out and be gone in a flash, and when you catch up with them and approach them, they will act mean and swim at you with their mouth wide open. They will bite too, and although their bite won't usually be as serious as that of a five or six footer, it will still hurt plenty. It's always best to handle them with care and not take any chances.

I needed some morays badly one time and was searching a likely area when I came to a huge flat rock, the type that I knew would house a moray. I took a deep breath, then swam down and placed my feet firmly on the sea floor and lifted the rock up to eye-level so I could see under it. Suddenly a huge spotted moray swam straight at my face. It veered slightly and went between my arm and my head and its tail caught me full in the face, knocking my mask off and giving me such a blow that for a few minutes my face was numb and I couln't tell whether I had been bitten or not. Catching morays with a small hand net is always an adventure.

One particularly hair-raising experience with a moray occurred in dirty water around a large coral head. I was diving on a large inshore reef, heavily populated with fish of every type, in about fifteen feet of water. There were huge schools of grunts, snapper, porkfish, and various species of jacks, and there were also multitudes of bait fish which attracted most of the other species. A tremendous school of silverside minnows swam about the reef, making it dangerous for diving, since these minnows encourage large predator fish to feed. But since my entire collecting area had been made into a park, I had to do my collecting on the inshore patches and had little choice of areas to dive in. There were a fair number of choice colorful fish on the reef and soon I had a number of butterfly fish, orange demoiselles, beau gregories, neon gobies, and angelfish in my basket. I was diving on a very large coral head, trying to net a spectacular townsend angelfish. With its brilliant orange, blue, and yellow markings, it is a prized specimen. I had the little beauty cornered in a small pocket in the coral head and was trying to work him into my net when something began obstructing my vision. At first, I assumed that my hair was hanging down in front of my face, so I kept looking at the angelfish through the lower part of the mask. Finally, I was running out of breath, so I backed off a foot or so from the coral to try and get a better view of the fish that I was trying to capture. Then I saw what was obstructing my vision. It was a huge, six-foot green moray eel! He had been right up against my face mask, looking at his reflection in the glass. When I saw what it was, I made a tremendous back flip and nearly wrenched my back. I see many of these dangerous eels but usually not quite so close. Had this fellow grabbed me about the face, not only would I have been horribly mutilated, but I could very easily have drowned. Not very many months before, I had read where a skin diver was dragged down into a deep hole by a green moray and drowned, despite the efforts of two companions who tried to free him from the eel.

Green morays grow to at least eight to ten feet and probably to twelve feet and although they are not poisonous, they are very dangerous to skin divers under certain conditions. They are very common and nearly every reef will house at least one or two very large green morays and dozens of the other species. On some reefs a single large coral head may contain twenty or more eels and they will bite a careless hand if they are cornered or in a feeding mood. The safest method to avoid an eel bite is to always assume that there is a moray under every large rock and proceed accordingly. Be especially careful around large coral heads for green morays since this is their usual hideout. Morays generally move from one part of a reef to another by underground tunnels, and sometimes when you are working under a coral head a large moray will come over to you from another section of the reef out of curiosity. You can see portions of their body slithering through narrow holes in the reef as they weave their way towards you. They usually prefer to travel this way rather than out in the open, being protected from large grouper or barracuda. If the moray is very large, it doesn't fear anything, least of all a skin diver, and it is the large eels, five feet or over, that are really dangerous.

Barracuda are another danger likely to be encountered by the skin diver, being very common on the reefs.

I would estimate that in the past fifteen years of diving, I have encountered close to half a million barracuda. I have seen them in shallow water less than two feet deep and in the blue waters of the Gulf Stream, and although I have had very few of them actually bother me, I can't say that they don't frighten me a little, especially the very large ones.

It's a known fact that barracuda attack a certain number of swimmers and divers every year. Sometimes the attacks are provoked, but often they are entirely unprovoked and may occur in very clear water. They are unpredictable. You may encounter ten thousand without incident, or you may encounter just one which will savagely attack you. When a barracuda attacks, it is with lightning speed, for they are among the fastest swimmers in the sea. They move through the water so fast that they almost become invisible, and if one decides to attack, you will have little chance of avoiding it.

It is true that most attacks by barracuda are a pure case

of mistaken identity. They are in a feeding mood and slash at you, mistaking a part of your arm or leg for a fish. This is especially true in dirty water where only the light por-

Giant barracuda are the true tigers of the sea and can move with lightning swiftness. I encountered a gigantic 8-foot specimen on one diving trip, and it was a frightening monster easily capable of biting a man in two. (Photo courtesy Marineland of Florida)

tions of your body show up from any distance and makes the 'cuda think it's a fish struggling in the water. If you wear anything shiny like a ring, bracelet, or watch, that glints or sparkles underwater, the 'cuda will slash at it, thinking it food. I have had them grab a pipe from my hands on two or three occasions and attack the shiny clamp on my collecting net as I rose to the surface. It is extremely dangerous to wear any shiny objects when swimming in tropical waters, for they definitely will attract predatory fish.

The largest number of barracuda I have seen at one time was on a Bahama expedition with Sid Anderson. We were swimming off the east coast of Andros Island in the beautiful clear waters when we encountered a tremendous school of young 'cudas that probably numbered in the hundreds or thousands. They were small, about eight to ten inches long, and the school seemed endless. The young 'cudas were being escorted by a very large 'cuda, who probably fed on them from time to time since he looked very well fed.

Skin divers often ask if the barracuda is really dangerous or if they can completely ignore him when they meet him on the reefs. I would say that if the water is clear, and the skin diver is not wearing anything shiny, nor spearing fish, and there are no small bait fish like silverside minnows or pilchards in the immediate area, the barracuda is of little threat. Barracuda are very curious and they will usually swim over to investigate a diver who invades their domain. They may resent his intrusion and make threatening passes at him, often gnashing their teeth or shaking their head as they swim towards the diver. This is quite unnerving, especially to a novice, and although they seldom complete the attack, one is never 100 per cent sure.

I think I can safely say that I have encountered 'cudas under practically every conceivable situation, and that their behavior is generally very much the same. First of all, contrary to some "experts," barracudas are not afraid nor can they always be easily frightened away. A large 'cuda just doesn't need to be afraid and he knows it. To him you

are a slow, clumsy turtle and he can swim circles around
you so fast that you can't even see him half the time. He
knows he has a set of jaws and teeth that can slice you in
two. It's true that sometimes you can frighten a small specimen away by swimming toward it rapidly, and sometimes
this also works with a fairly large fish, but remember that
it doesn't always hold true. In fact, it doesn't work most of
the time. If a 'cuda swims away, it's because he wants to,
and you probably had little or nothing to do with it.

Large 'cudas often travel in mated pairs. As with most
living creatures, one mate will protect the other, so that if
a diver shoots or even threatens one of the pair, he can
invariably expect trouble from the other. Or, if the fish are
spawning and a diver invades the area, he can expect trouble, for the fish will attempt to drive him away. One of my
closest calls with a 'cuda happened in this way.

I was collecting specimens and swam into a gathering
of a hundred or more 'cudas, which were apparently
spawning over a shallow bed of staghorn coral. As the
heavy females swam back and forth over the coral, the
males would swim in close to them, no doubt fertilizing
the eggs as they were dropped into the sea. (This is the
common spawning method of fish that do not build nests.
The fish lay their eggs in mid-water or near the surface
and the males swim close by and fertilze them as they drop
to the bottom or as they float through the water.) I was
watching them as I swam cautiously by when I noticed a
fairly large 'cuda several feet away. He was acting very
strangely. He was swimming around me and his eyes were
taking in my every move. His mouth was opened and he
was shaking his head in true 'cuda fashion. Then he
changed color, first taking on a light shade, then turning to
a dark color with broad bands. His eyes rolled up into the
top of his head and he curled his lips outward so that his

teeth seemed to be pointing straight forward like sabres; then he came at me at top speed! Usually a 'cuda starts his rush at a distance of ten feet and stops four or five feet away, but this fellow was starting his rush from four or five feet away. He headed right for me and was aimed right at my chest. At the moment of contact I arched my body and he missed me only by a matter of inches. He repeated his attack and again I arched my body so that he missed at the last second. I became quite unnerved, of course, because this fellow was clearly attacking me. I gradually swam away from him so that there was no mistake that he was the victor. He watched me intently as I moved from the area, and I am sure that he would have continued the attack had I stayed there. He probably thought I was after his mate, either to threaten her or as a rival, but he definitely did attack me, and if I had not seen him coming, I am certain he would have mauled me with his sharp teeth. It taught me a lesson, though. Whenever I see a great many 'cudas just milling about in shallow water, I give them a wide berth. If I have to dive there, I keep them in view at all times, and if any become too aggressive, I swim in the opposite direction and let them have the immediate area. After all, they were there first, and any sportsman should give them this consideration.

Barracuda are more likely to be dangerous when the tide is rising since this is when most large fish are on the prowl for food. Anyone who has spent much time on the bottom soon becomes aware of this, for the fish act quite differently when feeding time arrives. They are wary and alert and any sudden thrashing of fins or flippers will send the smaller snapper and grunts scurrying into the safety of the coral. I have learned to take advantage of this myself, for when I suddenly see all the small fish swimming rapidly into the protection of the coral heads, I know some large shark or 'cuda has invaded the reef and I quickly turn to face it. This has probably saved my life more than once. Spearfishing is especially dangerous when the tide is rising, and when 'cudas appear on the scene, the diver may be faced with an aggressive 'cuda which will attempt to snatch the speared fish from the very arms of the diver. This can

Barracuda are very common in Florida and Bahama waters and will usually not bother divers. I see anywhere from one or two to hundreds every time I go out. Never wear rings, watches, or shiny objects in the water, for 'cudas will bite savagely at these things, sometimes grabbing an arm or leg with them.

be very dangerous. If the fish is thrashing about, it may attract the 'cuda from a considerable distance away, and if he is hungry he will swim in rapidly for the attack. The fact that you are holding the spear will be of little or no significance if the 'cuda really wants the fish. Small 'cudas less than three feet can be frightened away, but the large specimens will not scare and could well unnerve you when they approach you with that hungry look about them. They will dart around you very quickly, their faces assuming a fierce expression. Then they will go into an evasive action that is quite different from their normal approach. When a large 'cuda swims in for a fish on your spear, it is best to let him have it, unless you are right near the boat, otherwise he may take it anyway. Don't try to shield the fish from him by holding it against your body, for he may take a part of you along with it. He knows what he is after and will take it one way or another. Sometimes you can save your catch by holding it out of the water as you swim toward the boat, but this is only recommended when the 'cuda is not really determined. You should, however, keep him in view at all times.

I remember one time in particular, while I was diving with my friend Rick Fried off Soldier's Key in Miami. Rick had speared a nice hogfish and was swimming back to the boat with the fish thrashing wildly about on the end of his pole spear. A huge 'cuda appeared and made repeated passes at the wounded fish. Rick held the fish out of the water so the 'cuda couldn't get it, and it then began to look as if the 'cuda was getting angry, for he began swimming madly about both Rick and myself. Fortunately, we were near the boat and Rick soon had the fish aboard, but it began to be a little tense, for the water was quite dirty, the tide was rising, and the 'cuda was clearly enraged. I became slightly concerned about my own safety, but luckily nothing happened. After all, who can really say that a 'cuda won't turn on a diver when deprived of a meal?

Spearing barracuda is not recommended for the beginner. It is not even recommended for the experienced diver, for many spearfishermen have been severely slashed by 'cudas they had speared. It is especially bad to shoot one with a spear that is attached to the gun by a strong cord. This is almost suicide, for if it's a large 'cuda, the moment he reaches the end of the line he will invariably circle around gnashing at everything in sight, and if the diver is close, he may find that 'cudas aren't really afraid of divers when two huge jaws clamp down on his arm or leg. This has happened to many divers and could easily prove fatal. The first large 'cuda I ever shot almost did this very thing to me.

I was in the Bahamas and was making underwater movies when a large 'cuda appeared on the scene. At first he was just curious about me, but then he became curious about the movie camera. He saw his reflection in the glass cover of the underwater case and began butting against the glass. I was somewhat of a novice at the time and thought the 'cuda was after me, rather than just being curious. He kept following me and gradually I got up enough courage to swim back to the yacht. I handed the camera to the mate and yelled for the speargun, which was an arbelette with spear and line attached. Before anyone could caution me, I shot the big fellow squarely in the gills. He swam rapidly away and was so strong that he actually pulled me through the water. I held on to the gun for a few brief moments, but let go when the mate on the yacht yelled, for if he hadn't seen what was happening, the 'cuda would most likely have turned on me with savage fury. I was glad I let go of the gun when I did.

Dirty water is the chief hazard with barracuda. If a diver

must work in water with poor visibility that is known to
contain 'cuda, he should be certain that he is not tempting
fate by wearing any object that is light colored or shiny.
Even the palms of the hands or the soles of the feet should
be covered. It's amazing how closely the soles of our feet
resemble a fish when in dirty water. The sun lights them
up, and often they are the only parts of our body visible
from any distance. The rest of the body being somewhat
darker and usually tanned will tend to blend in with the
murky water. Dark clothing and dark colored bathing
trunks are generally preferred.

It was in dirty water that I had an attack from a barracuda that could easily have been fatal. I was working one
of the shallow reefs off Garden Cove. It was winter, with
the usual sustained winds and murky water, but I had to
have specimens. The water was so riled up and dirty that
I could hardly see more than a few feet. I was catching
neon gobies, high hats, angelfish and porkfish, which I
would catch in close proximity to the reefs. The tide was
coming in strong and I became increasingly nervous, for
I knew it was both dangerous and foolhardy to be diving
under such conditions.

I was trying to net a small blue angelfish that had holed
up in a crevice in a large coral head, and I was thrashing
around in the water trying to stay down in the shallow
depth so I could catch the elusive little fellow. All of a
sudden, I turned around underwater to find myself staring
straight into the jaws of a huge barracuda. It wasn't especially long, probably about five feet, but it was extremely
heavy, being nearly a foot in diameter. It was right up
against me just a few inches away. My thrashing about in
the dirty water had apparently attracted it. It didn't do
anything especially threatening except that it was moving
about me so close that I could hardly keep from colliding

with it. There was only one thing to do. I took a firm hold of the heavy pipe I always carry and swung it down straight on top of the creature's head. I never expected to hit it for I thought it would quickly swim out of the way but I made a solid contact on its skull, which made a loud thud underwater. To my amazement the huge cuda drifted slowly away. It looked like I had either stunned it or killed it! I had never done anything like this before so I followed it out into the murky water hoping to retrieve it as a souvenir of my encounter. But it wasn't dead. Slowly it started to move. Then it shook itself a couple of times and veered off into the gloom. I could see that it was turning, for I caught a glimpse of its eye, so I instinctively held my collecting net in front of me. Suddenly the huge fish swam straight at me at top speed. It caught me full in the stomach and I could see the jaws flash sideways for that terrible, slashing bite. But miraculously I didn't even get a scratch. I was using a fairly large collecting net at the time, made of extremely tough plastic screen, and when the big fish attacked, I held it close to my chest and stomach. In addition, I was wearing a very heavy rubber suit with a lead-weighted belt to offset the buoyancy of the suit. It was probably the large net that saved me, for the 'cuda's teeth probably entangled in the screen enough so that it couldn't take a firm bite. At any rate it did give me a slight stomachache and scared the daylights out of me. The fish made only one pass, as if to reprimand me for hitting it on top of the head, but I didn't stay in the water long enough to give it a second chance. I'd had it for that day. The boat was only a short distance away (a rule I follow when working dirty water), so I climbed aboard fast and quickly examined my net and body for teethmarks. A 'cuda's teeth are so sharp that it can actually slash a diver severely, causing little or no pain for the first few minutes. But I suffered no wounds. The net had a few holes in it, but they would be easy to repair.

I related the incident to a few scientist friends, but I suspect they didn't believe it at all. Some of them have become so engrossed with so-called fact that they wouldn't believe anything unless they saw it themselves. Even then, they wouldn't believe it, because their mentors may have told them that such things don't happen. I know one scientist who flatly states that morays or barracudas will never attack a diver and that all the stories about such attacks are pure "adventure tales." He said that he has gone out and observed dozens of green morays on the reef and has never had one show any signs of aggression toward him. But I think he has a lot to learn. I have also seen dozens of morays, even hundreds or thousands, but I positively have had some of them attack me. I suspect the researcher had observed his specimens in clear water and he just didn't see enough specimens really to make such a rash statement. He should try working the giant coral heads in Hawke's Channel on a year-round basis, especially when the tide is rising and the water is murky. He may suddenly find something holding on to his leg and it won't be a mermaid!

The same is true of barracuda. Some so-called experts will adamantly state that the 'cuda is all bluff and that the diver has absolutely nothing to fear from them. The "experts" will descend on the reef from a huge 100' to 300' ship with all kinds of motors and gear. They will set off dynamite and spread poisons to get their specimens. I suspect the 'cuda would react differently under these conditions. Of course I do concur that most barracudas will rarely bother a swimmer or diver if he doesn't molest them, but I will categorically state that if you swim in even slightly murky water with a shiny brass anklet around your leg, sooner or later you will find that one of your legs is missing!

I have seen the barracuda at work. It is a swift and vicious killer. I have seen them slice through a large fish, bones and all, as though it were made of butter. They will come right up to a boat and snatch a fish from a line. One time we had a huge 'cuda attack a large bonito just as we were bringing it aboard. The 'cuda actually struck the side of the boat in its rush to get the prized food. When we brought the bonito aboard, only the head was left. The barracuda had knifed through the ten-inch body with one snap of its jaws!

As far as I am concerned, the 'cuda is a dangerous adversary, one to be treated with respect, never to be totally ignored. Chances are it won't bother you, but keep your eyes on it just to be sure.

7
The Mysterious Island

MY EARLY YEARS OF COLLECTING WERE FILLED WITH YOUTH-ful recklessness and wild abandon. I had absolutely no fear of sharks and barracuda. Large green morays were considered a challenge, something with which to do battle. I used to look forward to meeting a shark and would hit it on the head with a piece of pipe if it got too close.

The boats I used were rentals, most of them so decrepit they weren't fit to take to sea. The hulls were rotted and they leaked badly, making it necessary to start bailing almost as soon as I left shore. One in particular was so rotted that the entire stern came off the boat, with the motor still attached, when I had struck a shallow sand bar! Luckily the water was only a foot deep or I would have lost all of my gear. I simply stepped overboard, grabbed the forward part of the boat and pulled the two sections back together, pushing the rotted stern back into its proper place. Then I bailed furiously and gently eased the boat back to the dock. I told the old "conch" who had rented me the boat that the stern was "kind of loose" (trying not to laugh) and that he should tighten it!

One boat leaked so bad that I had to time myself while in the water, making certain not to stay too long or the boat would sink. When I climbed back in, there would be six to eight inches of water in the boat and I had to be extremely careful not to capsize it as I climbed in. It leaked so bad I would use it for a live well, tossing small sharks and morays into it while collecting, then gathering them up when I got aboard. The people who rented the boats took no care of them at all. Sometimes I would have to bail out as much as a foot of water before I could even load my gear. Then I would have to search around for an anchor, usually an old cement block. The Florida Keys were a wild and free place then and it was either take what was available or go without. It wasn't like the Keys of today where there is a boat dock at every turn of the road and a conservation agent looking down your throat every time you surface from a dive. It was a wild, untamed place where a diver could spend a week on the reefs without seeing another boat or diver except perhaps on weekends when there might be one or two boats on the horizon.

I dove every day, six days a week, rain or shine, except in the foulest of weather. I dove when small craft warnings were hoisted, when small boats were warned not to even leave shore; and I paid for it. I dove by myself most of the time. That part I didn't like, for it was terribly lonely. But it does give a man a chance to find himself and I found myself a million times over. I was making a living, a good one—but at enormous risk. The old men at the docks who came to know me and whom I had befriended, had warned me many times that sooner or later a shark would get me for diving out there all alone. I guess I sort of surprised them when I came back day after day, year after year with both legs intact.

Of course I did see sharks, hundreds of them over the years and a few of them did give me a bad time. I didn't mind them so much when they would circle me at a distance and make themselves known. It was sort of like meeting a friend or companion. All of a sudden I wasn't all alone out there. I would look at them and say hello to them through my snorkle. They would swim around me for a while to see what I was doing and then with a wave of their tail they would be gone and I would be alone again. I sort of considered them my silent friends under the sea. But the sneaky sharks I didn't like! They would suddenly appear from nowhere and be right up against my back, trying to crowd me. These would make my hair rise and my flesh crawl. I didn't consider them friends at all. They were cowards who couldn't face up to a fellow and it would make me unhappy to turn suddenly and find a huge mouthful of teeth and cold eyes regarding me as a possible dinner. It infuriated me! They would come in so close that I could hardly turn around without colliding with them and I would have to drop down and swim under them so that I would have room to maneuver. Then I would turn and face them and *dare* them to attack. I carried a heavy piece of pipe with me at all times and learned how to use it effectively underwater. I think that the very fact that I would turn and face the shark, rather than try to swim away, has protected me from attack.

But I wasn't the first diver to spend a lifetime alone in the sea. There were others before me and there will be others after me. I met one remarkable man, Bob Zimmerman, right on Key Largo, who had spent the greater part of his life under the sea, much of it all by himself. He had lived to a ripe old age, and nothing had ever happened to him, at least so far as being eaten by sharks is concerned. I rented boats from him for a number of years when I had switched my collecting from Garden Cove to Rock Harbor and he had told me that he had met many sharks in the water and that they never bothered him. He loaned me his own air compressor so that I could try it out on the reef with my collecting. It worked fine but I found that the air hose would get caught around coral heads just when I would be chasing a fish. I tried it for a while but then went back to just plain snorkling. I found that I could cover a much greater area, uninhibited by diving hoses. Perhaps in deep water where there wasn't too much coral the compressor would work better, but where I collected my specimens simply diving for them while holding my breath worked just fine. The biggest problem wasn't catching the fish, it was finding one the right size to collect. This sometimes took a considerable search.

The boats at Rock Harbor were much better than the old tubs I had rented before and eventually I bought a boat of my own which I kept at Garden Cove. I returned there for the balance of my collecting as it was a more lucrative area and the in-shore reefs were protected from the fury of the strong winter winds.

I found each day a new adventure, a new discovery. The reefs were never the same and each day I would learn something new about them. I carried a spear gun in the boat, not for protection, but to get a fish for my dinner and late in the day I would look about for a good-sized grouper or hog snapper, which I would shoot with little fanfare. It was much better fish than could ever be purchased at the local market. But in addition to fish I had lobster, succulent delicacies such as stone crab claws, blue crabs, shrimp, which would cost a small fortune in the quantities we had them. This is one of the fringe benefits of a marine collector. The other is the ever present possibility of finding sunken treasure, while poking around the reefs in search of specimens. I found dozens of wrecks while diving and met a number of treasure divers. In fact one of them, Marty Meylach, lived just a few blocks from us in Miami and had accompanied me on a number of trips even collecting marine fish for me at one time.

Everything about collecting is exciting and interesting. In my search for specimens, I explored the reefs from Miami to Key West, always finding something different. I dove off Big Pine Key, Looe Key off Marathon, Hens and Chickens Reef, Molasses Light and all the reefs north to Fowey Light off Miami. I don't know how I ever had the energy to survive my first ten years. For awhile, I was attending the University of Miami at night while diving on the reefs all day so it can be said that I put in a very full day, without any exaggeration. I would attend class so exhausted that I would nearly fall asleep, which would bring a slight reprimand from my pretty teacher, Miss Sudds. I would keep her informed of my daily exploits under the sea, the number of shark attacks and other adventures, with little notes at the top or bottom of our test papers. One time I told her that the reason I was late for class was because I had a blow-out in the center of the Seven Mile Bridge, was chased by a seventeen-foot hammerhead shark, and nearly lost my boat when it drifted away while I was diving. Her remark the next day on my test paper was, "All this in one day! My! My!" The little anecdotes continued through the class. It was a lot of fun. I didn't take a full college course but gathered up bits and pieces of an education as I had the time. Life just seemed too short to spend four years in school. I had tried it once at the University of New Hampshire and decided it wasn't for me.

One time my English teacher asked the class if anyone had had anything published. I didn't show my hand during the class but after class I told her that I had written a couple of books and a number of magazine articles. She of course wanted to see them but I asked her not to show them to the class when I brought them. She was most enthused about them and brought them around to the other teachers, who crowded around with numerous questions and comments. It seemed that none of the teachers had written a book and I felt a little foolish about the whole thing. She told me not to change my style of writing in any way. She was a very sincere teacher and I often wondered what happened to her. She probably settled down and got married, which happens to a great many people. I still have some of my test papers from the university with the little remarks by my nice teacher. It had been a lot of fun.

It seemed like I was the busiest person in the entire world. I was writing monthly columns for two magazines on salt water fish, collecting full time, and going to school at night. On top of that, I would get interesting collecting jobs that would almost stagger the imagination. Like the time I was hired by Marine Studios to lead an expedition to the Bahamas for an underwater movie venture. This was an exciting venture and I enjoyed it. Then there was the time that I was hired to explore a tiny island on the very outer edge of the Bahamas for a millionaire who wanted to purchase it and possibly get into the salt water tropical fish business.

I had been approached at my store by his business manager and then taken out to dinner in a chauffeur-driven limousine with six men, all firing pointed questions at me. I didn't know what to make of the situation. The whole thing had a secret, mysterious tone to it and I began to wonder if it was some type of nefarious plot to get rid of me. It seemed that they wanted me to go to this tiny little island, far out in the Bahamas and swim underwater around the entire island to make an underwater survey of the area. The whole project was hush-hush. In fact they told me that I must sign an agreement not to mention any part of the project for a period of five years! I began to have doubts about the whole thing and almost backed out a couple of times. It seemed strange that this group would come to me out of nowhere with such a strange proposition. But I always have had a flair for adventure so I decided to hear them out.

I would be flown to the island in a small, private plane and would be there for a week or two or whatever it took to complete my work. There was said to be a barrier reef around the edge of the island and most of my diving would be done inside the reef since the barrier was nearly a mile from shore. However, I would be expected to dive outside the reef if the weather permitted it. Eventually we got around to my salary for the job. I told them my usual fee for such work was $100.00 per day plus travel and expenses but they offered me $150.00 per day, which didn't bring any objections from me. Also, I requested that another diver accompany me as I didn't like diving in such a remote area by myself. This was agreeable with them and after the usual handshakes, the meeting was quickly terminated. They would contact me later for the actual departure date. Meanwhile, I should locate a diver to accompany me. They brought me back to my store and quietly drove away as mysteriously as they had appeared.

I called up my good friend Ken Howe of Fort Lauderdale and asked him if he would accompany me for a week or two of diving, all expenses paid as well as a salary, in the outer Bahamas. He was delighted. I told him I couldn't tell him the name of the island as I didn't know it myself and that the whole thing was secret. He would have to sign a paper to keep the project in strict confidence for five years. I told him that I would let him know when and where we would meet for the trip but expected it to be soon. He should have his diving gear ready and I would do the same.

A week went by and then I got a phone call about the trip. I was beginning to wonder if they had forgotten about it. I was told to be in Fort Lauderdale airport at 8 A.M. and to bring the other diver with me. We would fly in a small chartered plane to the island. I was reminded that I must sign the agreement not to divulge the purpose of my mission before I could get on the plane. In fact, if I didn't sign it, the whole deal would be off! I began to wonder just what I was getting into but decided to see it through to the end.

I met Ken Howe at the airport and shortly I was paged over the loudspeaker to go to the information center. I was greeted by one of the men I had met in Miami and introduced him to Ken. Then we were ushered to a small plane out on the landing strip. It didn't look like it would be large enough to carry us with our diving gear. Just before we got on the plane, I was handed the agreement to sign. I balked a little at signing it and was again reminded that if I didn't sign it the whole trip was off. I was assured that it was just a paper to keep the trip secret for five years and there was nothing more to it. It seems the client wanted the project to be confidential for business reasons. I finally signed the paper and Ken did also. Then we got aboard the plane. Despite its small outward appearance, it had six seats with luggage compartments in the wings. Our gear was loaded and in a few minutes we took off for the strange adventure. The plane was fast, almost like a fighter plane.

(The episode took place over 5 yrs. ago, so I can tell it now.)

In just a few minutes we were over the blue Atlantic and shortly we were out of sight of land. It was exciting and Ken was as excited as I, even though he knew absolutely nothing about our mission except that we would be diving for about a week around a remote island somewhere in the extreme outer Bahamas. After an hour or two, we were informed that the island was ahead of us. The pilot would fly around it a few times so that we could study the underwater formations from the air. It was indeed an isolated place and there were numerous outcroppings of reef at every turn. It looked like an interesting place to dive and we could hardly wait to land.

The pilot brought the plane into a small rocky landing strip that was none too smooth for it apparently had been used very little, and in a few minutes we were in the main lodge of the local hotel. Some natives had gathered around the table and the first thing they asked was about my proposed diving trip and if it had to do with the salt water tropical fish business which might be started on the island. Some security, I thought! The whole thing was supposed to be secret and every native on the islands knew about it. But then, keeping a secret on an island is nearly an impossible thing for every move one makes comes under close scrutinization since it becomes an item of interest to the otherwise dull routine of island life.

We were assigned a room at the lodge and then instructed to meet down at the dock for a trip to the island. I thought we had landed on it but we hadn't The mysterious island was some ten miles away and could only be reached by boat. We loaded our gear aboard a small launch and headed across the open water to a speck of land on the horizon. What we would find and do there could only be left to the imagination at this point. We were introduced to a Swiss professor, an ichthyologist or curator of some aquarium in Switzerland. He spoke no English so we couldn't communicate with him. But he was a very jolly fellow and we had a lot of laughs. He would do some diving and exploration also, we were told.

In a short while, we were approaching the island and were soon tied up at the dock. There was a beautiful home there, high up on a hill overlooking the lonely sea. Apparently the island and house were for sale and, in addition to my underwater work, I was requested to evaluate the land, trees and general habitat of the island and offer possible uses for them. We went to the house and went through it. It was beautiful and very well constructed of natural rock. It had beautiful fireplaces and had a commanding view of the sea in every direction. What a marvelous place to live, I thought.

After a thorough investigation of the house and the nearby land, we were told to help bring a large Boston Whaler from the house down to the beach for our diving work. The boat was in a shed beside the house and it looked like an impossible task to get it down the rocky hillside to the sea. But soon, a boatload of natives arrived from a nearby island and about twelve men simply carried the boat bodily over the rocks down to the beach. It was a very heavy boat but with all that help it was a cinch. The boat had a large outboard attached to it and this was carried along with equal aplomb. Soon the boat was in the water and the motor started.

We began our underwater survey. My client wanted me to examine the underwater potential of the island in regards to possibly setting up a salt water fish collecting station there. I was to make notes of the kind and number of all salt water fish in the area and include food fish as

well, paying particular attention to the exotic coral reef
fishes, which would be valuable if collected in quantity.

We headed out of the lagoon across the grass flats to the
edge of the reef and then Ken and I went overboard to
begin our study. The place was crawling with fish, especially large groupers and snappers. I never saw so many
good food fish in one place. It was an untouched tropical
paradise so far as a sports fisherman was concerned. There
were dozens, hundreds of grouper ranging from five or ten
pounders to huge monsters weighing well over fifty pounds.
Conchs were so plentiful that they were actually piled up
two and three feet high in places, not dead shells but *live*
animals. There must have been *millions of them.* In fact
there were enough conchs in the area to support a full
time business on this one product alone. I had been pretty
well all over the Bahamas but never had I seen so many
conchs in one area!

We snorkled all through the area searching for colorful
fish in particular as this was considered the most important item. There was a fair number of them but not near
as many as I had seen in other areas of the Bahamas. There
were plenty of food fish and conch but the colorful fish
were not too abundant. We saw a number of butterflyfish,
angelfish, rock beauties and other gems and as we moved
out from shore into deeper water we encountered the ubiq-
uitous royal gramma. These were very common once we
got below the fifteen foot depth. On the deeper reefs, we
would swim down to forty or fifty feet and grammas would
be seen in all directions as far as the eye could see. They
would swim upside down under the coral ledges. It was a
spectacular sight, as this is one of the most colorful and
stunning of all salt water fishes. We gazed in awe at the
tremendous number of them. We saw other desirable
marine fish suitable for the aquarium but there were not

really many of them compared to other areas. Also, we noticed that the water was quite cold even though it was very warm outside. At first we couldn't understand this but later we found that the island was far east of the warm Gulf Stream and didn't get any warm water from this important stream. We were out in the cold Atlantic.

Even while we were there, we noticed that many fish were cold. They would huddle together in groups under the coral ledges to keep warm much as they do in the Keys during cold weather. This explained why the colorful fish were not too plentiful. The water just wasn't warm enough for them. The seas were very calm and we headed outside the barrier reef for a look at the deep water. Ken is a superb diver and would swim down to sixty or seventy feet to peer under deep ledges for fish. We swam all the way out to the drop off where the water was too deep to reach bottom and noted all of the different species of fish, making notes on them as soon as we climbed aboard the boat. The fish were even less plentiful in the deeper water but this was to be expected.

We covered the area outside the barrier thoroughly. I didn't see a single shark. Then we worked back in towards shore stopping at every reef to record the marine life. There was a good number of fish on the reefs, of practically every type and description but they just weren't as plentiful as in other areas of the Bahamas. I made note of this in my reports. We rode completely around the island and dove until late to take advantage of the good weather. We could cover the surrounding islands in the following days to see what type of marine life existed there.

It was time to come in for dinner so we headed back to the lodge and a much needed rest. The manager told us that we were right in the middle of the ill-famed Bermuda Triangle where dozens of planes and ships had disappeared without a trace. In fact during World War II, a whole squadron of military planes disappeared in the general area. Even one of the search planes loaded down with all kinds of electronic gear and a twenty-four hour supply of fuel was lost without a trace, not a distress call or a single piece of wreckage from it or any of the planes was *ever found*. I shuddered as I thought about it for we still had a lot of diving to do in the area. The island was on the extreme outer edge of the Bahamas and once you left shore, there would be nothing between you and Europe should motor trouble develop. We kept in sight of the other boat at all times. It contained the professor and a couple of the other men who had come along for their own observations, mostly with glass-bottom buckets. Ken and I did most of the diving although the professor did go in the water from time to time.

We stayed on the island for about a week and covered the entire area underwater, making a complete survey of the reefs and fauna. I made up my report but did not give as glowing a report as my client had anticipated. I believe in telling things exactly as they are, which is how I did my report; but because it was not exuberant in depicting the colorful fish I think they were somewhat disappointed in my findings. However, I did point out that in warmer weather there would probably be many more reef fishes and also with a good boat or plane, side trips to better collecting areas could be made to supplement the local collections of fish. I read my report into a dictaphone and was instructed to file a written report when I returned to Miami. The recorded report was radioed back to New York that evening and the following day, Ken and I were flown back to Lauderdale in a small private plane. I thought we would hear more of the project later on and had hoped that it might turn into something big. We had become quite friendly with the men from the project while on the island and in fact they had even asked if we would care to work for them on a full-time basis. I declined but had told Ken to make his own decision. It had been a most interesting week and when I returned home, I promptly filed my written report as per our original agreement. I sent a bill for my services, which was promptly paid and never heard another word from the people involved. I did hear via the newspapers that they had purchased the island and that President Nixon became a frequent guest there, but never a single word about the project. Everything about the mysterious island has remained mysterious to this day.

8
The Virgin Wreck

ABOUT ONE WEEK AFTER MY NEAR FATAL ENCOUNTER WITH
the giant tiger shark, I had one of the most exhilarating
experiences of my entire diving career. It began when I
awoke one day to find the skies clear and no wind. It was a
perfect diving day and I just could not afford to miss it. I
called up a friend who wanted to go along to fish while I
dove, and an hour later we were headed for the reefs.

It was a perfect day with flat, mirror-like seas and not a
trace of a breeze. I was in my new Fiberglas boat, the
Queen Angel, and I opened her up full throttle. It wasn't
long before the blue waters of the Gulf Stream greeted us
and I began to look for suitable reef cover along the shallow edges.

I headed south a few miles to very shallow water at the
edge of the Gulf Stream and soon located an interesting
formation of fire coral and sea fans, which I knew would
hold a variety of colorfish, including the fabulous jewel
fish. The first thing that caught my eye as I descended onto
the reef were bits of wreckage scattered about the sea floor.
At first I didn't pay too much attention to it, but then it
hit me like a ton of bricks that I had anchored my boat
directly on a virgin wreck of ancient vintage. I had found

an untouched treasure ship! The full impact of it didn't hit me until I had swam about it for a half hour or so. There were cannons resting on the bottom and a six- to eight-foot mound of red building block, which was almost completely encrusted with fire coral. Scattered about the mound were many bits of wreckage showing green seepage, which indicated copper or bronze buried within the coral. On one side was a pile of objects, which at first I thought were kegs of cement or other useless material. They were about fifteen inches long and a foot in diameter. Projecting out of the sand was the keel. There were also many strange coral encrusted objects lying about. I was so excited I didn't know what to do or where to begin. I could tell that no one had ever probed it for treasure because the ballast rock and coral were completely untouched. Furthermore, it appeared that as the wooden hull slowly rotted away, the ballast rock had settled to the bottom in a lump, where it eventually became encrusted with coral. The cannons would also have been removed, since these items are in great demand by divers and archaeologists.

I picked up some heavy metal bars that were lying on the bottom and handed them to my friend, who was busy fishing. I had told him about the wreck, but since wrecks are very common on the Florida reefs, he was not too interested. The bars were heavy and we figured that most likely they were iron, but I wanted to take them home for further study. When I scratched them under water, they appeared to be silver, but apparently this was a natural occurrence with most metals. I also pried a piece of heavy ceramic pottery from the ballast rock, which looked very old and bore exquisite markings. It was getting late in the day, and since my friend had come along primarily for fishing, I felt that I was neglecting him with my continuous diving. I had collected a few jewel fish near the wreck, but he hadn't had so much as a bite on his line. I asked him to hand me a marker and I attached it to the wreck, planning to return soon with a diver and really explore it. Then we pulled anchor and headed out to the Gulf Stream

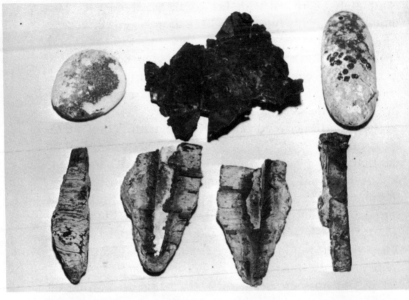

Typical round ballast rock found at the scene of old wrecks likely to contain treasure. Crumpled object at top center is copper sheathing used to cover hulls of ships. Bronze spikes are shown at bottom. Spike at left still contains remnants of old wood. Often the age and origin of the ship may be determined by the type of wood used in construction.

where we trolled for fish without success. It had been a beautiful day and the seas remained almost flat during the entire trip. The sky was clear and the air was warm. It was a perfect day to spend at sea. The sun was getting low and we were about thirty miles from the dock, so with reluctance I opened the throttle and headed for home.

That night I poured over my books on treasure hunting,

and the more I read, the more excited I became. I called up my good friend Russ Smiley to see if he would be interested in joining me. When I told him of the wreck and the possibility that it could easily contain treasure, he was very enthusiastic and we made plans for a trip on the very next day. I had just read of the many millions of dollars in gold that was lost off these very reefs and never recovered. Russ, an accomplished author of marine life, agreed that this could be a real find. It certainly was worth immediate investigation.

The next day we met at the dock, loaded our gear into the boat, and headed out to sea in the highest of spirits. The radio had predicted calm seas and no rain was forecast for the entire day. We got an early start and since the seas were still moderately calm, we were soon across the bay and approaching the reef markers. I had planned to follow the route I had taken the previous day, which I felt would bring us to the marker on the wreck. I had noted that the wreck was very close to the Gulf Stream, so as we headed south from the reef marker, we stayed close to the drop off where the water becomes very deep. Then we strained our eyes for the small marker I had tied to the wreck. Our hopes were high and we had planned and envisioned ourselves working the wreck the night before, even discussing what we would do with the gold or silver if we found any. Of course we also realized that the wreck might not contain a thing, but at least we knew we could get interesting artifacts for our homes.

A gentle breeze began to blow and an hour passed quickly. We thought we had sighted the marker several times, but when we approached closer, it turned out to be sundry floating objects. We still had high hopes and pressed on with the search. The seas began to roughen and soon a fair breeze was blowing. Waves bagan to build up to four feet. White caps formed all around and clouds began to hide the sun. Soon visibility became impaired by the sea, which began to churn into angry waves. Since we were so close to the Gulf Stream, the sea began to get quite high and soon we were battling five- and six-foot waves. I had been battling fierce winds all winter, which had completely ruined my collecting (I had only about five good diving days in four months). I became angry at the seas and pressed on with the search for the wreck. I was determined to find it, come hell or high water. The high water came and we began to encounter seven- to eight-foot seas. Russ kept commenting that if they didn't crest we would be alright because as long as the waves don't break, the boat simply rides over them. When the seas are rough on shallow reefs near the Gulf Stream, the waves usually rush over the reefs in giant combers, which can easily sink even the stoutest vessels. Fortunately, the tide was high and the waves weren't cresting, at least for the moment.

The wind began to blow very strongly now, and it was becoming increasingly difficult to see, as we were constantly bombarded with waves that invariably caught us square in the face. The waves were building up to dangerous heights and the tops were starting to curl into crests. We looked shoreward to find a gigantic storm covering the entire horizon. Jagged streaks of lightning cut through the sky and huge clouds began scuttling over us at great speed. I reminded Russ that the radio said there would be no rain and we both laughed as we had been fooled by that favorable forecast so many times in the past. We decided that we had better head in, the faster the better. The wind was picking up to almost gale force and we could see tremendous sheets of rain already pelting the mainland. We knew we could never make it to shore ahead of the storm, since it was rushing out to meet us at top speed. Russ suggested that we run into Sands Cut and wait out the storm there. Every so often, a huge wave would break over the bow, sending a deluge of water across the windshields but the boat took the seas well and I was thankful that I wasn't in the old boat I had used so often in the Keys. I felt the first drop of rain just as we reached the safety of the Cut. We pulled up to the mangroves and tied the boat tightly to the protective shore. Then we secured all the canvas awnings and the rains came. It was a real tropical deluge. The wind roared over our heads and the rain came down so hard that we couldn't see but a few feet. We were thankful to be in protected water instead of out on those stormy seas. We were quite disheartened that we hadn't found the treasure ship. It was almost a classic climax to a treasure hunt—divers locate treasure only to be thwarted in their attempts to recover it by the weather. We drank coffee and waited for the storm to abate. The rain lasted nearly an hour and was highlighted with a blast of heavy hailstones which pelted the boat like pebbles.

The main portion of the storm finally blew over and the sun came out. The weather appeared to be calm again so we started the motor and maneuvered out into the channel. I was very depressed at not finding the wreck and I know Russ was also. During the day, I had described the entire wreck to Russ many times, each time adding a little detail that I had missed before. We began to almost visualize gold bars and pieces of eight. It was almost too much to bear. Then we thought of the possibility that what I thought were kegs of cement might actually be chunks of treasure chest, in which the chests themselves had rotted away, but the treasure within had fused together and become encrusted with coral. It was entirely possible. During my years of diving, I had encountered many treasure divers and gradually pieced together a fair knowledge of treasure hunting. I knew that treasure is usually encrusted with all types of marine growth so that I never expected to find any out in the open. My wreck looked exactly like those described by experienced treasure hunters. Not to be able to find it again was frustrating beyond words. I still hadn't given up for the day, and as the storm passed by, Russ and I rode back and forth up the small channel in the Cut debating whether or not to go out again. We almost tossed a coin to decide, but then we noticed more storm clouds building up near shore, so we decided it would be more sensible to head in and try again in the near future. It's just as well that we did, for the bay was very rough and the wind blew in strong gusts all the way to shore. We unloaded the boat with heavy hearts, but vowed to try again very soon. I had promised my two children, Paul and Julie, a piece of the pirate ship, but they realized that the storm had ruined the trip.

Next day, I awoke early and listened to all weather reports. I called Russ and we decided it was too windy, but after an hour had passed, I called him again and told him that the wind hadn't increased and that it would probably be a fairly good day out on the reef.

Once more we made the trip. I followed the same route as before and really combed the area, traveling a good twenty miles to be certain that I had not missed any section. Word must have spread about my find, for there were skin divers all over the place, many of them clearly searching for something. Two airplanes cruised overhead and I suspect one or two boats were actually following us. I was extremely fearful that someone else would find the wreck before us. We painstakingly combed the entire area back and forth all day without success. The marker must have come loose or someone had found it and removed it, or we certainly would have found it. We headed for shore again with heavy hearts and our dreams began to fade. We were still determined, however, to find the wreck even without the marker. We decided to give it a number one priority over all other work. We would pick a calm day and drop markers after we covered an area until we located the wreck. I was determined to find it again. When I returned home again that day, I looked at the piece of ceramic and the iron bars. I also had a piece of the red brick with fire coral attached so that I knew I hadn't imagined the whole thing. There was a real, virgin treasure ship out there just waiting to be explored. I found it once, and if I didn't find it again, I felt I would go mad. I had gold fever. I knew that the chances of really finding buried treasure are very remote, but I had been diving almost constantly for the past ten years in the very area where the treasure ships were know to have gone down. Unlike the occasional diver who goes only on weekends, I dove several times a week, all year long, so that my chances of finding treasure were as good or better than anyone else in the country, or even the world. A treasure hunter had once told me that there is very little treasure on most of the wrecks about Florida, as they have been pillaged for many years. But, he added, if you ever come across a pile of ballast rock, especially the red brick, that is completely overgrown with coral, then you have a real find that could easily contain gold bullion. This is exactly what I had found and more, for my wreck had cannons, what could be pieces of eight all lumped together, and the actual keel of the ship protruding through the sand. When I think that I was probably staring at a million dollars in gold that day, as I first dove on the wreck, I almost become ill.

9
Gold!

THE WIND BLEW STEADLY FOR THE NEXT WEEK AND THE treasure ship haunted me day and night. At night I would toss and turn and listen to the wind howl through the trees outside my windows and I would feel sick inside, for as long as that wind blew I knew I would have to stay ashore. All kinds of thoughts ran through my mind and I pictured other divers exploring my wreck and removing all the treasure. I was becoming more and more depressed. I almost began to wish that I had never found the wretched ship.

Finally, the wind abated and the weather report predicted smooth seas and clear skies. This was the day I was waiting for and I could hardly restrain myself. I had filled two dozen small bottles with yellow paint and would toss these overboard with rope and weights when I reached the general area of the wreck so that we could methodically cover the entire reef area until the treasure was located. I also had some large markers that I could attach to the bottom if I found the ship. I certainly did not intend to lose it again if I ever came across it. I loaded all my gear into my car and called up Russ Smiley to see if he could accompany me. Unfortunately he had business to attend to and couldn't make it, so I decided to go by myself.

It was a perfect day and the seas were nearly flat calm as the weather broadcast had predicted. Visibility was unlimited and I was in a happy, optimistic mood. I really didn't think I would find the treasure ship, but my hopes were high. I decided I would follow the exact same course that I had taken on the day I first located the wreck and see if I could stumble across it again. Soon I had reached the blue waters of the Gulf Stream and I lined up a Coast Guard marker with the blue waters and headed south slowly as I had done on that first day. I was very careful, turning slightly one way and then back again on course as I headed south. I let the boat guide itself in the general direction of where I thought the wreck might be and closely scrutinized the color changes of the water ahead. When I first located the wreck, I had noticed a shallow, white area ahead of the boat and found the wreck as I headed for the shallow area. My heart quickened when I saw a shallow, white area ahead again and I slowly turned the boat toward it. The water under the boat began to shallow and then I saw a large, dark area directly ahead. I was becoming very excited now and when I reached the dark area, I knew at once that I had found my treasure ship again. My joy knew no bounds! I was so excited, I could hardly wait to get into the water. I quickly threw the anchor overboard and scrambled into my diving gear. Then I was in the water and gazing upon the elusive wreck that I had tried so hard to find. It was exactly as I had left it, except that the marker I had placed there was gone. I must have failed to tie it tight enough, I thought. But now it didn't matter. I would make all kinds of land and sea fixes, so that I would be able to find my wreck again.

The water was crystal clear that memorable day and I swam about surveying the site, hardly knowing where to begin. I finally decided to dig around the large pile of ballast rock, reasoning that this would be the most likely spot for treasure. I had a small hand pick and it worked perfectly for digging in the sand and removing small rocks. As I dug, I would uncover brass nails, pieces of colored pottery, brass spikes, and other small items that marked the remains of an ancient ship. I noted that there were several large cannons and that they were almost completely overgrown with coral. There were also several piles of ballast rock. Some of the rock was round or flat granite, while other pieces were red clay brick. I came to the conclusion that perhaps there were two or even three ships piled up in this one area. The location of the wreck was right on the edge of the Gulf Stream and at the edge of deep water, so that a ship could easily hit it during a storm. It was in a peculiar location, which explained why I was unable to find it on my other trips, as it was away from all the other reefs. It suddenly jutted up out of deep water, which explained why it had remained quite unmolested for hundreds of years. Or so I thought at first until I sighted pieces of deep sea diving hose scattered about the area. Some diver had worked the wreck, but that had been a long while ago, for the diving hose lay partially covered with sand and lay under huge chunks of rock. A chill went through me as the thought struck that perhaps the diver had perished while exploring the wreck, for it seemed unlikely that he would leave his diving hose behind. I cut off a chunk of the hose and put it in my basket for further study.

Then I began to explore around the old cannons. I chipped away small chunks of encrustation and soon hit black metal, which I knew was iron. I found a long bar under one of the cannons that gave off a silver glint when I pierced it with my hand pick. I scraped it with the flat edge of the pick and it glistened bright silver. All of the

The author examines an ancient piece of wood dug out from the coral rock at the sight of the virgin wreck. It was a solemn occasion. (Photo courtesy Russ Smiley)

other metal was powdery black when I probed into it. This particular piece was also in the shape of a long bar. My eyes grew wide with excitement as I further uncovered the bar. It was well imbedded under the huge cannon and I worked feverishly to free it. I was snorkle diving so I had to make repeated trips to the surface for air. The water was only about ten feet deep, but I was taxing my strength by trying to stay under too long. I just had to have that silver bar and I dug and pounded with my hand ax until finally I wrenched it free! Nearly completely exhausted, I swam back to the boat and placed the gleaming bar on the diving platform on the stern of the boat. I was so tired and weakened that I could hardly climb back into the boat. I rested for about an hour and then picked up the "silver bar" and examined it closely. It wasn't very heavy and I began to wonder if it was really silver. I had been fooled many times before.

The weather was still perfect and after I had rested, I drew diagrams of the wreck from above the surface, so I could recognize it easily from a boat. I also made note of its relation to several points on shore and checked its exact distance from the Gulf Stream. I didn't want to lose the wreck again. I began to feel more rested and decided to work on the wreck some more, this time at a more leisurely pace. The water was still clear and warm and I was having a happy and enjoyable day. I examined the strange drum-like objects and tried to dig into them with my pick but they were extremely hard. I managed to break off small chunks from the edges and whatever the objects were, I am sure they contained some type of metal. They were so heavy that I could not lift them off the bottom, even though they were only about fifteen inches long and a foot in diameter. They would bubble and hiss loudly when I dug into them an inch or two, and they seemed to contain some type of copper colored metal mixed with some sort of black material. I couldn't figure out what they were, but I did not see any signs of silver or coins, so I assumed they were of little value and went about exploring other sections of the wreck.

There was a considerable amount of wreckage scattered over an area of about a hundred and fifty feet. The remains of one vessel protruded out of the sand and strange shapes of coral indicated that parts of the wreckage were growing right into a coral reef. I was picking at small encrusted areas to determine whether it was coral or metal when I made a most amazing discovery. I had been searching around the edge of an old cannon when I discovered a faint outline of what looked like another cannon coming up through the reef. I picked at it, and as I flaked off a chunk of coral, my eyes opened wide. I had discovered gold! I picked furiously at it and soon had uncovered a glistening gold object about a foot across. I was flabbergasted and could hardly believe my eyes. When I surfaced for breath, I looked down and the gold object sparkled, as the sun reflected on it in the clear water. I had uncovered many brass and copper objects before and they were always tarnished or coated with green, but this thing was completely untarnished. When I removed the coral crust, it shone brilliantly as though it was brand new. It had to be gold! The immediate thoughts of immense riches began to pour through my mind and I felt that I had struck it rich at last. My strength was suddenly renewed and I decided to concentrate all my effort on the gold. But the sea does not give up its treasures easily and I worked all the remainder of the day, trying to remove the huge gold object from the bottom of the sea. It was imbedded in solid coral rock and would not budge, even the slightest fraction of an inch. I worked for hours on it, trying to get it loose, but to no avail. Then, I tried to cut a piece of it loose, but this was impossible with my limited tools. I had only a small hand pick, an ax, a hammer, and a screwdriver. I tried to cut a corner off with the screwdriver, but could not swing the

As I probed the old wreck with a hammer, I suddenly uncovered a bright gold object nearly a foot across. Note the round ballast rock in foreground. (Photo courtesy Russ Smiley)

hammer hard enough under water to cut through the metal. The metal itself was rather soft and dented easily with the pick ax, but I couldn't cut through it. Finally, I noticed that the sun was hanging low in the sky, so I decided to chip off some small pieces so that I would have something to take back with me to have analyzed. As I chipped at the gleaming gold object, dozens of wrasses and blueheads would swarm in and grab the glittering chips, as they cascaded through the water. I never thought I would see fish feeding on gold, but there they were, gorging themselves on my treasures. I finally succeeded in picking up three small quarter inch long chips of the shiny metal and carefully carried it back to the boat, inside the thumb

The brilliant gold covered object uncovered on a wreck in the Florida keys gave the author weeks of anxious moments. It was embedded in rock and coral and rested under a huge coral-encrusted cannon. The author believes it to be a vase or urn of some type.

of one of my gloves. Then, reluctantly, I covered the shiny metal object with rocks, so that no one else would find it and I returned to the boat where I briefly looked over my day's collection. I had accumulated a fine assortment of brass spikes, some pottery, the "silver bar," and some other small objects but my prize possession was the three small chips of shiny gold that I held in the palm of my hand. These three little objects could well change my whole life, I thought.

I pulled up the anchor and headed for a Coast Guard marker on which I had taken a compass bearing. Then I ran the boat at selected rpm, timing the distance from the wreck to the marker. This would give me another way to locate the wreck should I have trouble finding it by shore points. Satisfied that I could find the exact spot again, I headed home at top speed, dead tired but very excited. It was after dark when I finally reached the dock.

That night, I called my friend Smiley and told him that I had found the wreck again and of the gleaming gold object, swearing him to secrecy. He was as excited as I was and we made plans to retrieve the treasure. He couldn't make it the next day, which was just as well since I was too worn out, so we made definite plans for a full day's assault on the reef the following day. We decided·to bring aqua lungs, a heavy six-foot crowbar, extra rope, hammers and other gear. Also, I would bring my underwater camera to take photos of the big event.

I had already told my friends, Claire and Lawrence Holloway, who happened to be in town, since I was anxious to have their advice on the best procedure to follow in retrieving and disposing of the treasure. Of course they were very interested and they came by the house to look at the bits of wreckage, pottery, brass nails, and the piece of diver's hose I had cut from the wreck. Finally, with a dramatic gesture, I produced the plastic vial with the tiny chips of gold. Lawrence looked at it carefully, weighed it in his hands, and suggested that I put some acid on it. He said if it was brass, the acid would eat into it, but if it was gold, the acid would have no effect on it. The more I talked about the wreck, the more details I could recall.

When I described the shape of the gold object, it puzzled everyone, for we couldn't figure out what it could be. Then the thought struck me that perhaps it was the brass faceplate of the ill-fated diver who had somehow perished in the wreck while searching for treasure. The thought also occurred to me that perhaps his air hose was purposely cut after he had handed the treasures to his partners up on their boat. It was a grisly thought, but it certainly could be true. Lawrence examined my tiny samples closely and said that they looked like gold but didn't seem to have the weight. He said, though, that he wasn't sure and that I should take them to a jeweler, one who didn't know me, and find out for certain. Claire and Lawrence both cautioned me about mentioning that I had found gold to anyone if it turned out to be the real thing, for they said people would follow me home and even out to sea when I went to get the rest. I joked about becoming a millionaire and told them I would call them if I found out my little samples were the real thing.

After they left, I looked about the house for acid and couldn't find any. Then I remembered that the car battery contained acid, so I carefully removed some with an eye dropper and put a few drops on the shining chips of metal. I observed it with a low power miscroscope to see if there was any reaction. The acid had no effect on it whatsoever! I put a few drops of the same acid on one of the old brass spikes I had taken from the wreck, and it bubbled furiously. Yet, when I put more on the gold metal, there still was no trace of a bubble. Surely, I thought, my metal must be pure gold. I called Lawrence on the phone again and told him of the acid test and he said it was a good indication, but to take it to a jeweler to be sure.

The next day I busied myself by filling my aqua lung tank with air and had my regulator checked. Next, I made a visit to several jewelers with my tiny gold colored samples, and, after examining the metal with a file and magnifying glass, they were uninamous in exclaiming that it was really gold. Several coyly asked me where I had found it, but of course I wouldn't divulge my secret. One jeweller was very nice and said he hoped I would find a big chunk of it. I became more excited with each appraisal and by the time I reached home, I felt as though I had really struck it rich. Russ had asked me to call him when I found out about the samples and when I told him it was the real thing, he whistled and became very excited. He said he would like to go out with me that next day, come hell or high water, and that he was so excited that he wouldn't be able to sleep. I told him to be certain not to tell anyone about it.

Then I called up Lawrence and Claire Holloway and excitedly told them the news. Claire told me not to breathe a word about it to anyone or I would start a real gold rush and have every boat in the entire state out combing the reefs for gold. Lawrence said I better get a gun and keep looking over my shoulder. He said if the thing I described out there was solid gold, it would be worth a fortune, and if people knew I had it, many would try to take it from me. Claire ended our conversation with a grim reminder that I had better be very careful out on the boat and for me to be sure to call her when I got back from the trip, so she'd know I made it back safely. I told her I would, and as I hung up the phone, I began to wonder if finding a huge chunk of gold would bring me nothing but trouble and misery, even if it did bring me wealth. Maybe I would be better off to leave it out there and forget that I had found it, I thought. But it was one of the most exciting things that ever happened to me and I decided to go through with it. I felt I should get the gold first and then worry about disposing of it.

Russ Smiley called and said he had the heavy crowbar, a new rope, and the rest of the gear and that he would like to drop by my house and see the artifacts and gold chips I had found. He said he would come by in the evening on his way home from work.

By now, gold fever was running through my veins and I couldn't think of anything else except that huge chunk of gleaming gold sitting out there on the bottom of the ocean. I would be exuberant one minute when I thought of all that gold that would soon be mine, then I would be almost frantic the next minute as I thought that perhaps at that very minute some diver was out on the wreck carefully removing my treasure. I felt like rushing out to the reef that very afternoon, and even mentioned it to Russ when he called, but we decided to wait until morning and put in a full day with our aqua lungs and other equipment. Russ and I had jokingly mentioned gold fever before and how we would be fighting each other down on the reef if we found some real treasure, and although we were just joking at the time, I began to visualize that something like this could actually happen unless we made a firm decision as to the actual handling and disposition of the treasure before it was found. I decided that since I had found the treasure, I should have the final say on what we did with it, so I drew up an agreement in duplicate expressing my wishes.

That night Russ came by and I showed him the brass nails, pieces of pottery, and other items I had brought back from the wreck. I saved the tiny bits of gold until the very last and then finally brought them out. Russ looked at them in awe and asked me again how big the chunk was out in the ocean. I told him it probably would weigh several hudred pounds and he could hardly contain himself. We sat around the dinner table and I casually brought out my agreement. I told him it was just between him and me and that I would like him to look it over. I said that I felt it would eliminate possible trouble and misunderstandings later on. He read it and said it was very fair and generous, and then we signed it to make it somewhat official. We discussed the gold object in detail, wondering what it could be. I felt it was some sort of a large urn or vase and, if this was the case, we figured that perhaps we would display it around the nation as a rare gold artifact and lease it to museums and art shows. We felt this would be more profitable than selling it and that we could probably make a permanent income from it this way.

I had some heavy chunks of coral rock, which were imbedded with greenish colored objects, glass, and tiny chunks of pottery, that I had taken from the wreck, and Russ and I spent an hour or so out in the garage, carefully breaking them with a hammer. We thought that they might contain pieces of eight or jewelery, but they contained nothing more than broken glass and strange bottles an inch or two in length. I also showed Russ my "silver bars." They were badly rusted now and a magnet clung to them, so we knew they were simply iron. But the gold was the important thing .Who cares about silver bars, I joked. I also showed Russ some of the ballast rock I had brought back and he agreed it was from a very old ship. The night was wearing on and we decided to turn in as early as possible, so we would be well rested by morning. We both knew it would be difficult to sleep.

After Russ left, I took out the tiny chips of gold again and put them on my desk on a piece of glass. Then I got some more acid and tried the test again. The gold was still completely untarnished and when the acid was applied, it didn't give off a single bubble, even under a thirty power microscope. I wanted to try the test again for I had told the jewellers I had given the gold the acid test and since none of them gave it the test, I wanted to be sure that I was correct in my diagnosis. But the acid test revealed no reaction at all, just as before. Satisfied that it was real gold, I closed the vial and then tried to go to sleep.

The wind had calmed down, and now instead of being frustrated because it was blowing, I was frustrated because it had calmed down. In fact, the whole day had been calm and I could almost picture divers working on my wreck and taking all the gold. I wondered if the secret had leaked out. Perhaps a telephone operator had told her family, or other skindivers had got wind of my secret. Maybe we would get out to the reef to find everything gone. I slept fitfully that night and woke up several times, the gold filling my mind like a nightmare. I wondered what the future would hold for me, now that I was about to become a millionaire. I had decided that day that I would immediately give up my fish collecting business, as I had become quite disgusted with it. All kinds of thoughts went through my mind and I fought for sleep. Finally, I let myself relax and, before I knew it, dawn had come.

I ate a quick breakfast and hurried down to the boat. I had loaded the car the night before so that we could get an early start. Russ was already there waiting for me so we quickly loaded all the gear, casting furtive glances around us lest we were being watched. I shook hands with Russ and said,

"This is the big day. Tonight we might be millionaires."

"Let's go get it," Russ said excitedly.

It was a beautiful day. The seas were calm and the wind was very slight. We headed out across Biscayne Bay and I joked with Russ that I hoped I could find the wreck again.

He joked back that I had better find it. I assured him that I felt we would, since I had made all kinds of shore sightings and lined up markers with points on shore, but I pointed out that sometimes it's difficult to find a place far out at sea even when you know right where it is. There were no white caps that morning and soon we came to the first Coast Guard marker from which I ran a measured course due south. Our hopes were very high and Russ said he had confidence that I would find the wreck, but we were both apprehensive as the measured minutes slowly went by. I concentrated very carefully as I had done the last time and soon the last thirty seconds of my measured timing were approaching.

"It should be right up ahead," I said to Russ quietly. "The shore markers are lining up perfectly."

The excitement began to swell up inside us, but we didn't want to become too excited until we had actually found the wreck. That last half minute was filled with suspense and as the shallow water appeared up ahead, I felt as though we were right on course. Now the two shore points were in perfect alignment and directly ahead I could see a large dark area; without a word, I headed for it. Then, we went directly over it and I said to Russ: "Well, here it is. Throw out the anchor, quick!"

Russ took a quick look with the glass bottom bucket and said he could see the square bricks from the ballast rock and also parts of the wreckage. We just couldn't wait to get into the water. We made the anchor fast and then scrambled into our diving gear and prepared to go into the water. We had decided to first look at the area with mask and snorkle and then figure out the best method for getting the gold loose. We would put on our lungs later.

I decided to take Russ on sort of a "Cook's tour" of the wreck before we did anything as I wanted him to see my virgin wreck before anything was touched. We went into the water and were soon staring at the elusive treasure ship. It was a thrilling sight. I showed Russ the huge piles of ballast rock and the strange drum-shaped objects that I had thought might be pieces of eight all fused together. I also showed him the huge cannons lying scattered about. Then, as usual, saving the best thing till last, I brought him to the spot directly over the gold.

Everything was exactly as I had left it on the previous trip. On the way out we had watched for boats that might try to follow us, but there had been none. When we had come to the general location of the wreck, there were no boats in the area and when we finally anchored, I was relieved that no one had found the treasure ship. Now, as I was about to uncover the huge chunk of gold, I felt that it was all ours. There wasn't a boat in sight. The water was clear and calm and I wanted Russ to see me uncover the gleaming object. I surfaced for a minute and said: "O.K. Russ, now watch this. This is the gold."

Then I swam to the bottom and began removing the boulders I had placed on the treasure on my previous visit. There it was, a dull yellow square-cornered object project-ing out of the coral rock. Russ swam down and examined it closely. Then surfaced and exclaimed: "That's gold al-right. It's got to be. There is nothing else that would stay underwater that long without tarnishing. It has to be gold."

The sun was still low in the sky, so that there wasn't much light on the sea floor and the gold object was in the shade. Still, it shone but it didn't glisten like it did when I found it. It had been late afternoon and low tide when I first uncovered it and the sun was shining directly on it so that it shone like a polished mirror. Now it was high tide and early morning and the light was still poor. Nevertheless, we were convinced it was the real article and we began debating what the best way would be to remove it. We lowered the huge six-foot crowbar into the water plus a smaller bar and a hammer. I had my hand pickax and I started to clear out the coral near the cannon. We had just begun to pry on the cannon with the crowbar when I heard a boat approaching. I surfaced immediately and Russ did also. We watched a small boat approaching from some distance away. At first it looked like it was going to head out to sea, but then it turned and headed straight for us. There were four skindivers in it and our hearts sank as they came within hailing distance. I mumbled to Russ to pretend he was just looking at the reefs while I tried to chase them away. As their boat approached, we saw them lower a glass bottom bucket and peer at the bottom about fifty feet from us. I was becoming frantic. If those skin-divers ever saw that huge chunk of gold down there on the bottom, there would probably be a fight to the finish. I had to chase them away.

I swam toward their boat with my hand pickax in one hand and when I got within yelling distance, I asked them what they were doing coming so close to us. I told them there was the whole ocean to dive in and to move on to another reef. They were determined to dive, and as we talked some of them were already putting on their diving gear. I had to act fast or they would find our treasure. I asked them how come they wanted to dive right next to us when they had the whole rest of the world to dive in, and told them it wasn't sporting to anchor right next to our boat, especially since we were there first. But they were determined to dive and I was just as determined to drive them away. Finally, I swam over to their boat and climbed part way over the side. I asked them again what their idea was, and one of them explained that they wanted to dive

on the very spot we were on and had waited for weeks for
the weather to settle down. They asked what we were
doing there and I told them that we were taking photos.
They promised they wouldn't get in the way. They said
they had been coming to the wreck for several years and
were bringing home the red ballast rock to build a fireplace. I thought to myself that this was quite a yarn and
that they were really after treasure. Finally, one of them
wanted to know if we had found something there and
that's why we didn't want them to dive. I assured them we
were just taking pictures and I went back to Russ who was
guarding the gold by swimming directly over it. He said I
shouldn't be too bold or they may think we really found
something and be all the more determined to stay. I asked
Russ to start covering the gold while I argued with them.
Meanwhile they had circled away, apparently deciding
among themselves whether they would stay or leave. They
came back, so I swam over and asked them to please stay
out of our way so we could get pictures and they agreed. I
swam back quickly while they were getting anchored and
helped Russ cover the gold. We decided to take turns
guarding it in the water and if one of the intruders tried to
uncover the gold, we would stop them. We didn't want
them to get a glimpse of it, feeling it would surely bring
trouble. The water was getting very cold and we were
beginning to get chilled so we took turns swimming over
the covered treasure.

We watched the divers get into their gear. They were
using aqua lungs and they carried small crowbars. We felt
certain they were searching for treasure. However, they
did pick up the red bricks and began carrying them back
to the boat. Every few minutes one would pass close by, his
aqua lung giving warning that he was approaching, for the
labored breathing could easily be heard under water.

When a diver did approach close to the cannon under which our gold was buried, I would swim to the bottom and pretend to be madly digging on the opposite side from where the treasure was buried. Then I would heave the rocks over the cannon onto the buried gold, making the pile larger and larger. The diver would glance curiously as he swam by, but there was nothing there to arouse his suspicion except the huge hole we were digging. We explained to them that we were looking for artifacts that might be buried there. One of them offered to help us, but I turned down his offer, saying that it was several days' work and that we were simply going to try to loosen the cannon on this day.

The water got colder and colder and Russ and I changed shifts every half hour or so. The intruding divers gave us no trouble and while I was resting in the boat, I asked them about the wreck. They said that there were at least two ships that had been wrecked here. I asked if they had found any treasure on the wreck and at first they said no, but later on, as the day wore on and we became friendlier, one of them said that they had found a silver teapot and a solid gold comb as well as silver spoons and interesting pieces of pottery. They said that several years ago a diver had worked the reef and left his diving hose behind when it became entangled in the reef. He had dynamited the wreck in search of treasure, they informed us.

The water was becoming increasingly cold and the wind was picking up, so on my next turn at diving I moved the anchor from the pile of ballast rock directly into the muzzle of the cannon beside our treasure. I reasoned that the divers surely wouldn't dive around our anchor. My dreams of a virgin wreck were shattered, but still we felt there might be treasure. We knew that at least we had one huge chunk of gold, and as we watched the intruders work on the bottom, we could tell that they were amateurs and probably wouldn't recognize treasure unless it was lying right out in the open. The wind was picking up and the water was becoming quite rough. We predicted that the

Author's floating basket and innertube is tossed about by wildly churning seas at height of treasure hunt. Black speck at left of innertube is Russ Smiley snorkling over the wreck.

unwelcome divers would not stay very long. When a diver uses two tanks of air in choppy water, it is quite tiring and with the seas picking up fast, we felt that it wouldn't be too long before we would have the wreck all to ourselves again. Our prediction proved correct and gradually the divers began returning to the boat. We made a few casual remarks about the wind getting worse and soon the divers began making preparations to leave. Some of them were very inexperienced, because one of them surfaced excitedly beside me when a large barracuda swam by. He said that it was the first time he had ever seen a barracuda and wanted to know if it was going to attack. I told him that it was only curious and that it wouldn't bother him. He seemed relieved, but he stayed near the boat after that. The wind was growing much stronger now and heavy swells began pounding on the shallow part of the reef. Our unwelcome companions bid us farewell as we jokingly told them that we wouldn't take any rocks if they wouldn't take any cannons. As they left we both got back aboard the boat for hot coffee and a brief rest before we began our final assault on the gold.

This time we put on our lungs, deciding to expend all our energy on retrieving the gold before looking for anything else. We took turns digging and lifting with the heavy crowbar, but we couldn't budge the gold object even a fraction of an inch. It was buried directly beneath a huge iron cannon, and, in addition, it seemed to be encased in a granite rock or in iron. We dug and hacked at it for hours and used up all our energy to no avail. I took my camera down and made a few pictures of the wreck and ballast rock and Russ took one of me actually digging on the gold. The water was not too clear, but we had no choice. At least we wanted some pictures of the treasure. The seas were becoming very rough now and the boat was tossing wildly with huge, crashing swells. We had to tie the boat with two ropes in addition to the anchor or it would have been swept away. Every hour or so a rope would break and we would have to re-tie it quickly before the other ropes gave. The waves began to get higher and higher and soon huge breakers were forming. They would hit the reef and send spray crashing twenty to thirty feet into the air. We were anchored just at the edge of the shallow reef so that the breakers would miss us but we got all of the rough water. The water became very turbulent and it took much effort just to swim against it. I was determined to get that chunk of gold, for now that other divers had been there I felt they

Huge waves nearly engulf the author's boat *Queen Angel* during the quest for pirate gold. Three anchor ropes were needed to hold the boat in place while we worked on the wreck.

would return and find it for certain if we did not get it on this trip. Russ didn't feel too good—he had just recovered from a very bad case of flu—but still he did a tremendous amount of diving. The ocean was getting extremely rough now and the sun was starting to hang low in the sky. I began to feel that we would not be able to get the gold object loose and our hopes of becoming millionaires had dwindled considerably. I began diving frantically in that last hour, but it was no use. That huge gold object was firmly entrenched in the ocean floor and we decided it

Gold fever made us endure violent seas while trying to extract treasure from the deep. Here a huge wave nearly swamps the author's boat.

would take several sticks of dynamite to loosen it. The sea was now so rough that it was ridiculous to remain any longer. Every time I would surface from a dive, I would emerge into a sea of white foam and would be so twisted around that I was becoming dizzy. Finally, I decided it was no use. We would have to call it quits for the day. I decided to at least pry off a chunk of the gold so we could have more to work with than the tiny chips. I stuck the huge crowbar under a corner of the gold object and lifted up with all my strength. The corner started to bend and finally it broke off. I swam back to the boat with it and gave it to Russ. He said he was glad that at least we got a piece of it for identification. Then I swam back to gather the tools and untie the boat. I pried off another small chunk so that Russ could have a piece and wearily crawled into the boat. It took extreme effort to lift the heavy crowbar out of that wild, churning sea. I couldn't swim to the rear of the boat with it, so I handed it to Russ from the bow. I don't know how he ever got it aboard and down through the bow hatch in that wildly pitching boat, but he did, for when I climbed aboard, he had it on the rack where it belonged.

We were both thoroughly exhausted as I headed the boat towards shore. Once more the sea had defeated us. We made it back to shore just as darkness fell and for our day's work we had each a chunk of gold. The larger chunk which was a corner of the gold object weighed about four ounces and I took that piece with me, planning to have it analyzed when we got back. We were still not absolutely positive that it was gold, for although the jewellers had stated it was, none of them had actually tested it. Our next step would be to determine for certain by actual analysis if the metal was gold and, if it was, then we would return to the wreck right away with more equipment. Russ said he was going to downtown Miami the next day and he would take his sample directly to a jeweler for complete analysis. He said he would call me as soon as he found out for certain. We loaded our gear into our cars and went home, thoroughly exhausted.

I called Russ the next day and he said he had taken his sample to a jeweler, but he wouldn't know for two or three days whether or not it was real gold. The suspense was killing me, so I called up some gold dealers in Miami and

The old wreck here little resembles a sunken ship. All that remains is the ballast rock and an occasional outline of the ship encrusted with coral and sea fans. The author has found the remains of close to a thousand ships in his years of diving in the Florida and Bahama waters.

one assured me that if I brought my sample down he could tell me immediately whether it was the real thing. An hour later I was in his office and hopefully handed him the gold corner. He opened a small vial of powerful acid and put a drop on the sample. It boiled furiously!

"I'm sorry," he said, "but it's not gold."

He showed me some real gold and when he put the powerful acid on it, there was no reaction. I felt sick inside. I asked him if he could give it another test to be certain. Then he placed the sample on a ceramic block and

Tons of round granite ballast rock usually mark the remains of old sunken vessels. Pieces of pottery, brass spikes, artifacts, and occasionally gold or silver may be found around or beneath the rock.

applied heat from a small torch. It melted only under very intense heat. He informed me that gold has a low melting point and that he was certain my sample was not gold.

With a heavy heart I left his office and went home very dejected. I decided I would have to go to work again after all. I called Russ and told him the sad news and he was very disappointed. He said his daughter had already spent his first million. He took it like a good sport though, and we joked about it a little although it wasn't really very funny. The gold expert had told me that many jewelers can't tell gold from brass, which surprised me since the jewelers had been so sure my samples were genuine.

Russ and I made another trip to the wreck a short time later to look under the ballast rock, but we didn't find anything except a few more brass spikes and other small objects. I explored the wreck with other divers later on, but, although we combed the area, we found nothing of

The casual observer can easily swim past a very old wreck, for unless he is accustomed to reef formations, there is little to identify a wreck except for the odd coral shapes or an occasional glimpse of ballast rock. Modern steel ships are easy to identify since portions of them stay intact for many years.

value. However, I still feel that the site could hold treasure. There is such a tremendous pile of ballast rock that it
must have come from several ships. The entire reef seems
to be made of granite rock and some is buried far beneath

This spectacular underwater garden is another world waiting to be
explored. Just seeing this fairyland is enough "treasure" even if
you never found any gold. (Photo courtesy Paul Tzimoulis)

the ground. The last time I visited the wreck, the gold
colored object was still there, but the wreck showed evidence that many divers had been there since my first visit.
One time while I was there a salvage boat with huge
booms and dredging equipment came to the area, but it
didn't stop since we were on the location. I still wonder
what the gold colored object could be and why it fooled
us and the jewelers.

Russ and I decided that we couldn't do any more salvage

on the ship without major equipment, so I wrote to Mr. Edwin Link of National Geographic, sending him a photo of the gold colored object and a few pieces of pottery. His office replied that he was out of the country but would contact me upon his return. If there is any treasure under the tons of ballast rock, it would be a major task to find it and only a large boat with proper equipment and trained help could accomplish anything.

Although I didn't get rich, I learned a lot about wrecks and treasure, for during the periods when I couldn't go out, I read every book and article on treasure diving that I could obtain. The venture was a disappointment, but it was exciting and I shall never forget it. I went back to work, catching my aquarium fish and figured that they were actually more valuable than gold and easier to dispose of, besides. Here was treasure for the taking and it wouldn't bitterly disappoint me. I was making a good income, was completely independent, and could come and go as I pleased, beholden to no one. My taste for treasure hunting would stay with me, though, and now I would be more alert than ever for the old Spanish galleon that might suddenly come into view as I drop anchor on some little explored part of the coral reef. Maybe the next one will have the gold bullion.

10
Living Treasure

WITH THE POSSIBLE EXCEPTION OF PIRATE GOLD, WHICH IS extremely difficult to find, the skin diver can be rewarded financially far more by collecting the small colorful reef fish for the millions of aquarists throughout the world. In fact, if a man has any business sense at all, he can make more income from collecting marine tropicals than by any other type of undersea work, and enjoy it besides.

Keeping saltwater fish is becoming one of the nation's most fascinating hobbies. In fact, I feel that it is destined to eventually overtake the freshwater aquarium field in the near future, for saltwater fish are much more colorful and intelligent, and the public is becoming aware of this very quickly. Many of the most common marine fish are more beautiful than the most exotic of the freshwater types, and the marine hobby has reached the stage where it is no longer difficult to keep the dazzling, highly colored beauties in an aquarium. As more freshwater hobbyists switch to saltwater, the need for marine fish will rise sharply, which will give skin divers an opportunity to make extra income from their sport, or make a fulltime living if they choose. Skin divers will soon realize that this living gold is far more accessible than the old yellow metal and can be

I swim down to a shallow reef and catch colorful fish with my hand net and "poker," a flattened piece of pipe. Gloves should always be worn when working around coral. (Photo courtesy Paul Tzimoulis)

converted to cash far more easily. A good fish collector can make a handsome living if he is willing to work hard and deal honestly with his customers. Of course, like everything else, it takes experience and know-how.

Divers must first learn which types of colorful fish are in demand, and then they must learn how to catch them. This is not quite as easy as it looks. But, if a man is a good diver, he can learn the basic rules rather easily and then with practice and patience, he will become a proficient collector. The simplest way to learn is to go out with a diver who has experience and watch how he does it. The first fish you catch may be the most difficult one; after that it will become easier with practice. The main object is to learn the habits of the fish and know how to approach them. Proper equipment is also important. Colorful fish may be caught in any type of small hand net, but some types are better than others. My first collecting nets were store-bought ones of white nylon, and although I caught a few fish with them, I soon found that they tore easily on the sharp coral. I discovered that if I made the net out of plastic screen it lasted much longer. I found that this was the ideal material for collecting nets. Its gray color was less conspicuous in the water and its stiffness proved to be a boon. The soft white nylon would wave back and forth in the current, which would frighten the fish away from the net, but the plastic screen was quite rigid and kept the net open. Since the current wouldn't sway the material, the fish would often swim right into the open net. I believe I was the very first diver to use this material in collecting nets and to date have found nothing that works as well.

The best all-around size for a hand collecting net is about a foot in diameter and about fifteen inches deep. The frame should be flat on the bottom and rounded at the sides. This will allow you to rest the net flat on the

The author examines a huge formation of rare pillar coral off Andros Island in the Bahamas. (Photo courtesy Paul Tzimoulis)

I found that the real gold on the reefs was the spectacular specimens, such as this gorgeous Queen Angelfish and butterflyfish.
(Photo by James W. LaTourrette)

bottom when chasing fish into it and the rounded sides will help when you work around large corals, making the net easier to maneuver than if it was square.

Basic equipment needed to catch "living treasure" is a good face mask, swim fins, black neoprene coated gloves, snorkle, and a "poker." This last piece of equipment is almost as important as the net, for without it fish collecting would be difficult and your hands would suffer many painful stings from long-spined urchins, which abound everywhere on the reefs. The poker is simply a piece of ½″ to

Live coral is becoming a prize for the collector who wants something different in his aquarium. Certain species thrive in home tanks and are easy to collect.

¾″ heavy galvanized pipe about eighteen inches long. One end is flattened for prying or probing crevices, and the other contains a smaller ¼″ thick piece of rod about six inches long. This is placed in the pipe, which is flattened to hold it, and the end is sharpened to a dull point. The poker is used to move sea urchins out of the way when you are chasing a specimen, usually with the flat end. Then, with the urchin out of the way, you can set your net in

Quarter-pound chunk of "gold" which started the author on a wild gold rush. Samples in vials at right were said to be gold by four jewelers and a mineral expert. Author feels that the object he discovered was a bronze urn dipped in gold.

place and chase the little fish into it using either the poker or your hand, whichever works best under the circumstances. The sharp end of the poker can be used for spearing urchins for bait when you want to chum fish, or for spearing a lobster for the dinner pot if legal. The poker also acts as a weapon, and will prove very useful in dis-

Spruce or Spiral Worms look like tiny blossoms on the coral. Touch one and it will disappear instantly into the coral. They live very well in the salt-water aquarium.

couraging the large green moray eels who may become too aggressive if you don't drive them back down into the coral when you first sight them. Sharks and 'cudas can also be discouraged by a blow on the nose if they get too close. Quite often you can drive them away permanently by throwing your poker into the air so it will land on their back. This frightens them, for something coming at them from out of the water is unnatural and usually causes them to leave the area for a long while. The poker is such an important part of collecting that care should be used in selecting it. A fairly heavy piece of pipe should be used so it has weight and strength; old galvanized pipe is best, since it doesn't have shine too much and doesn't rust too badly in salt water. Never use bright aluminum or brass, for this will attract large barracuda and they may attack you when biting at the shiny metal.

I have had this happen several times, and on two occasions the powerful snapping jaws of the 'cuda missed my hands by only about an inch. You can also use the flat part of the poker for prying loose a choice piece of brain coral from the bottom by inserting the flattened edge under the base of the coral and prying upward. And, of course, if you come across bits of old wreckage, your poker will prove useful for hammering at encrusted objects to see what kind of metal is concealed beneath. In fact, your poker will prove so valuable to you when you learn its many uses, that you will be lost without it. It's best to keep several in the boat in the event you lose one.

An inner tube with a wooden bushel basket lined with fine plastic screen will make a floating live well in which to place your specimens as you collect them. It also will serve as a safety float in case you tire or get a cramp. A length of nylon rope with a lead weight of about a pound may be attached to the tube so you can tow it with you along the reef. When you find a suitable collecting spot, you can drop the lead to the bottom and go after the fish.

The above equipment is all you will need to catch the beautiful living gems of the sea. Practically every type of interesting sea creature can be captured by snorkle diving. It is less tiring than lung diving and considerably more sport. There is hardly a fish on the reefs that I haven't been able to catch by holding my breath and diving after it. It's a real challenge to your skill, and when you have netted a choice marine beauty after a strong chase around the reef, you will feel quite elated that you had outwitted a fish in its own element.

This strange, long-nosed fellow is a sharp-nosed puffer, quite common on the reefs and an aquarium favorite.

The most important single rule in collecting marine fish is to learn where you can and cannot collect them. This may mean the difference between success and failure. Certain types of reef bottom are entirely unsuitable for collecting live specimens, and as you dive you will learn more about this. Staghorn or elkhorn reefs are almost impossible to work for tropicals since your net becomes entangled in the sharp coral and it is nearly impossible to corner a fish in

Nothing can match the beauty of a salt-water aquarium except perhaps a beautiful woman.

The author with his basic gear: mask, snorkle, collecting net, and rubber suit for winter diving. (Photo courtesy Claire Holloway)

the dense clusters of coral. Also, reef areas with dense rock or brain corals with huge crevices that join the corals together will be unproductive since the fish will simply retreat into the deep holes and there is no way you can get them out.

The best areas to work are around the edge of the reefs near small isolated coral heads. Dead coral reefs with numerous small rocks are excellent, as are gorgonia patches with just one or two coral heads. In these areas it will be possible to corner a fish and drive him into your net.

Quite often colorful fish may be caught in very shallow water, especially in the warm summer months. They may be found around rocky shores, near the edges or channels, and in the shallow sponge beds, especially around finger sponges. This last houses the exotic black angelfish, butterfly fish, and sometimes the highly colored queen angelfish. The adult fish spawn over this particular type of sponge and the young fish take refuge there. For this reason, it is extremely important that the sponge is not broken, for if you destroy the home of the fish you will ruin the area for years to come for yourself as well as for other divers, not to mention the fish. It is unfortunate that this interesting sponge grows in shallow channels, for in the Florida Keys many of the shallow channels have been dredged out for boats and the sponge forever destroyed. This will no doubt happen in due time to the entire Keys chain, from Soldier Key right on down to Key West.

It is not necessary to break or damage the coral to capture a choice specimen if you will exercise a little patience. Just watch the fish you wish to catch for a few minutes before you dive on him and learn his little pathways. Reef fish have special routes they travel as they swim about the reef, and when they are pursued they unerringly follow these paths to escape. Quite often if you carefully place your net in the center of their path and set it so it is open and erect, you can chase the little fish right into it on your first dive. This is especially true with angelfish and butterfly fish.

Graceful French angelfish (Pomacanthus paru) is easy to approach underwater and is an ideal subject for the underwater photographer.

Queen angelfish nearly always live under a large piece of coral or in a ledge, so if you come across one of these spectacular beauties, approach him from the large coral or ledge if possible and place your net so that his retreat back to the ledge or coral is cut off. Then with a little luck and skill you will be able to catch him before he gets into his hideout. It is usually easiest to catch a fish on your very first dive, especially if you have observed the movements of the fish before you descend on him, for if you miss him the first time, the fish learns to fear you and your net, and will quickly become aware you are up to no good. It is

Strange trumpet fish (Aulostoma) poses in front of a beautiful gorgonia in which the odd creature often hides when pursued.

amazing how quick a fish can learn that you are after him and can remember this for several weeks afterward, especially older fish.

When you have spent a few thousand hours on the reefs, you will get to know many of the fish, for you will find that some fish will pick out a certain piece of coral on the reef

The common toadfish lives in holes, empty beer cans, or wide-mouth bottles. It has powerful jaws and can inflict a painful bite. Skin divers should wear gloves when exploring the reefs and should not put their heads in holes or crevices.

and stay there for as long as a year or more. You will be able to watch small angelfish mature or see friendly grouper in the same holes, month after month. When you are collecting fish, you will find specimens that are too small, but if you remember where they are, you can go back a month or two later and chances are they will be right there and probably the right size.

The most popular Atlantic tropicals are rock beauties, angelfish, butterfly fish, red cardinals, cubbyu, neon gobies, jewel fish, blue reef fish, royal grammas, spanish hogfish, pearly jawfish, razorfish, beau gregories, demoiselles, jack-knife fish wrasses, banded coral shrimp, and arrow crabs.

The most popular pacific fish are lion fish, clownfish, blue devils, species of dascyllus, Pacific angelfish and butterfly fish, and small colorful trigger fish.

In general, most aquarists want small fish from 1″ to 4″. Large fish are sometimes needed for public aquariums or

The sargassum fish is one of the easiest of all fish to capture and one of the most fascinating to keep in your salt-water aquarium. It lives in floating sargassum seaweed and is easily captured by dipping up the weed in a net and shaking it over a bucket. The fish is the same color as the seaweed and hard to distinguish from it at a glance.

ordered by private individuals with very large home tanks. In addition, many types of invertebrates are also wanted, such as anemones, crabs, urchins, starfish, and small pieces

The basket starfish is one of the most unusual creatures in the sea and can sometimes be found under rocks and coral. If you encounter one while diving, put it in shallow water where you can watch it and see its intricate construction.

of live coral. There is so much interest in the sea and so many interesting things that can be kept in the aquarium that the list could go on and on. Even marine plants are in demand.

Aquarist and diver, Claire Holloway, looks at a queen angelfish in one of the aquariums in the author's store in Miami.

The important thing to remember when collecting is not to damage the reefs. It is not necessary, and if many divers cause excessive damage to the reefs, restrictions will be placed on collecting and, before long, most if not all phases of skindiving will be severely hampered or completely prohibited. There have been some very unfortunate rumors spread that fish collectors go out with crowbars and tear the reefs completely apart to get at specimens. This has done irreparable harm to the collectors and is totally untrue. I don't know of a single fish collector who uses a crowbar to tear up a reef to get his specimens, and although I have written hundreds of letters to Florida conservationists, senators, and other officials, they apparently believe this to be fact since it was first brought to their attention by a marine biology professor who, in their opinion, is considered reliable.

There have no doubt been some coral collectors who use a crowbar to obtain their coral since this is about the only way to get coral loose from the reef, but I have watched some of them work and they did not wantonly destroy the reefs. They were merely gathering a product of the sea. Actually, if coral is picked carefully, it can be harvested year after year, for it continues to grow. Pieces can be pruned from a reef and several months later a new leaf will form where the piece was removed. Five or six years later the entire wing will have grown back to its original size. What happened down in the Florida Keys was a strange turn of fate. A group of scientists got together and banned coral collecting in an area thirty-three miles long. Then along came hurricane Donna which destroyed more coral than had ever been collected. Many people can't skin dive and the only chance they ever have of seeing the beautiful handiwork of nature's reefs is when they see a piece of snowy white coral. Also, of course, many aquarists throughout the nation want coral for their aquariums. I feel that some restrictions should be placed on coral if it becomes scarce, but if divers use good judgment when they collect fish and coral and try to avoid damage to the reefs, there will be coral for all.

Keeping your saltwater fish alive and in good health will require skill and experience. A few simple rules here would be not to crowd the fish, keep them in the shade, and furnish aeration if possible. A battery operated pump with air stones will help a great deal. Use plastic pails or large plastic waste baskets and be especially careful not to get any oil in the water (you will lose your entire catch).

It is best to find a market for your fish before you collect them, since they should be sold as soon after they are collected as possible when they are in the best health and have the best color. If you plan to go to an exotic tropical

With salt-water aquariums even live corals or delicate tube worms may be kept and will provide months of educational enjoyment. Gorgonias at left also keep surprisingly well.

island for your vacation, contact your local pet shop and see if they want any marine beauties. They can usually furnish you with plastic bags to bring the fish back in and will give you instructions on the best way to handle the fish en route.

If you strike it rich and make a good haul with expensive marine beauties, don't brag about it too much, especially on the island where you are getting the fish. As soon as people think you are making money, they will find some

The star-studded marine jewel fish (Microspathodon chrysyrus) is a true gem of the sea and a living treasure which awaits the collector. It is, however, a difficult fish to capture.

reason to hinder or stop your project. It's the same as when you find gold: keep your mouth shut. Take your find home and quietly dispose of it. Then you can do it year after year and no one will bother you. If you collect wisely and don't damage the reefs, you can catch fish for the rest of your life and so can your grandchildren, for there are many dense, inaccessible reefs that will continue to produce colorful gems, which will overflow to other areas. Unless man steps in and allows wholesale drugging or poisoning of the reefs, there will always be plenty of marine beauties for generations to come.

The real joy in collecting "living treasure" will be if you catch them for your own aquarium and not for profit. Then you will have the supreme thrill of outwitting the beautiful little creatures and, after your hard day's work, you will be able to sit back and see the wondrous creatures you caught with your own hands. It's one of the greatest

Baby nurse sharks make wonderful pets for home aquariums and are easily captured by grabbing them by the back of the head. They are found under coral heads or large sponges. The young are handsomely spotted, but the spots disappear as they mature. Fang-like protruberances are soft barbels, a sensory organ.

joys of skindiving. Once you turn it into a business, it becomes work, and much of the joy and thrill is taken away. So, unless you need the money, do it for fun.

When I presented the world famous diver Captain Jacques Yves Cousteau with a copy of my book on salt water aquariums, he smiled and said: "This is something I am really interested in. It's much more of a challenge to catch the little fish than the big ones."

As the country grows, there will be more large public and private aquariums constructed, and collectors will be needed to supply them with live specimens. It's interesting work, fun at times, but there is a hard part to it. Old Man Weather plays a major role in this type of work. Wind is your most hated enemy and in the warm climates the wind blows a great deal. Winter diving is no picnic, and there is more demand for live specimens during the winter, so that a full-time collector must often work under conditions that are far from ideal. It can be trying work when the weather gets cold and the seas are rough and murky. Sometimes it makes you wonder if it is worth the effort. But in warm weather when the water is crystal clear and the skies are blue, the call of the reefs can be like a lodestone drawing the diver into the depths of the fascinating underwater world. You are certain to find treasure in this fairyland if you spend any time there. You most likely won't find gold, but the living treasure is always there. Use it wisely and it will reward you with knowledge and wealth. The challenge, the physical exertion, the chase through the coral forest and the triumphant feeling when you have finally netted a colorful gem for your own home aquarium is worth more than all the gold in the sea. When you get home and put the little fish in your aquarium, you can enjoy his beauty for months or even years and every time you look at the dazzling beauty, it will remind you of the thrilling

undersea adventure when you caught the prized specimen.
No other hobby can offer this.

The spectacular dragon fish or lion fish (Pterois volitans) is one of
the most unusual fish that may be kept in the marine aquarium. At
one time these wondrous creatures sold for nearly $500 each. They
come from the Pacific and Indian oceans.

My Workshop
Is the Sea

FOR TEN YEARS I MADE MY LIVING AS A MARINE COLLECTOR, diving for the most part by myself. At times it was incredibly beautiful and I felt carefree as a bird, but other times I felt so alone that words could hardly describe my feelings of desolation. Winters were the worst, because the bitter cold water and the gray skies took much charm out of the reef, and the sudden appearance of a large shark was always more depressing when the water was cold and murky.

One of my closest shaves with death was due to simple carelessness and was so close that I shudder just to think of it. I was collecting colorful fish on a shallow reef, and had chased a spectacular beauty into a hole just the size of my hand. I needed this particular specimen badly, so I did something I seldom do; I pushed my hand far into the hole to frighten out the fish. I noticed that the opening was a very tight fit and I began to wish I hadn't put my hand into it. I started to extract my hand as I was running out of breath when I realized to my horror that it was stuck tight! In those few anxious moments I realized what a foolish thing I had done. I looked up and could see the surface just seven or eight feet above and I tried desperately not to panic and use up those few precious seconds of breath still within me. It was such a pathetic situation I felt like crying. I thought how some of the men on shore would won-

Thanks to modern technology, the all-glass aquarium has become a reality. This will be a boon to the salt-water aquarist who was formerly plagued with rusty metal frames, corosion, and toxic cement in the standard aquarium. This handsome model with birch base and light hood was made by Ellis Skolfield.

der why my boat hadn't returned and would probably find my lifeless body anchored to the shallow reef and tell my friends what happened to me. I had no knife, and if I had, I would probably have tried cutting myself loose. I was wearing the cuff type canvas gloves, and those were what caused the trouble. The extended cuff of the glove had gone over a stem of coral and the opening was so small that

The coral reef is my workshop. I learned its secrets intimately and explored the coral wonderland by myself for half a lifetime.

I couldn't remove my hand from the glove. My lungs began to burst and my life began to fade as I let out my last few breaths of air. Everything turned red, then black, then dizziness began to overtake me. I was like an animal caught in a submerged trap, destined to drown. I had only mask and snorkle and already I had been submerged several minutes. I seemed to get a second breath, then a third breath, then that was all. My body went limp, my vision blurred, and in one last desperate attempt, I pushed my arm far into the hole and wrenched it back with all my strength. It came free! I surfaced and gulped in air and

My home for ten days was this beautiful 103-foot yacht, which cruised the delightful Bahama waters. I was tour leader for Sid Anderson's Bahama venture, which really was an adventure. Only one engine worked and the other was held in place with jacks, but we all had a marvelous time.　　　　　　　　　　(Photo courtesy Paul Tzimoulis)

Sid Anderson peers into a hole in search of grouper. Sea Fans and plumes give the appearance of the sea floor but it is actually the flat surface of the huge ship that sank off Andros Island in the Bahamas. Note extreme clarity of water. Visibility was about two hundred feet.　　　　　　　　　　(Photo courtesy Paul Tzimoulis)

then rested in the boat and thought how good it felt to be alive.

Night diving had always held a certain fascination for me and during a ten day trip to the Bahama Islands, in which I was hired as seminar leader by Sid Anderson on his marvelous, well-organized, Bahama Venture, I had the opportunity to explore the reefs at night from the comparative safety of a huge 104 foot diesel yacht. Mr. Anderson had brought along a portable ultra violet light for studying the fluorescence of various corals at night. The instrument was encased in a waterproof bag for diving and I was very anxious to try it. I had just finished working with the famous scientist Dr. Paul Zahl on an article on fluorescent sea life, which he was doing for National Geographic in which he photographed corals with ultra violet light in aquariums at Key Largo.* It was amazing how the corals would glow with weird colors under the ultra violet rays and I was anxious to try the light on an actual reef.

During seminar, which I gave each morning, I announced that we would have a night diving expedition and nearly everyone was interested in participating in it. However, by evening enthusiasm waned when it was pointed out that it would be a little dangerous since sharks feed at night and the area we had chosen to dive in would most likely be visited by sharks after sunset. It's a known fact that sharks venture in the shallow water close to shore to feed at night. This was further emphasized by the mate, Wayne Albury, who grew up in the Islands. He said he wanted no part in the "bloody mess" and he didn't even want to be close enough to the screams when the sharks attacked. The number of participants dwindled, but a fair number still wanted to see what the underwater world looks like when most of the fish have gone to sleep.

* *National Geographic*, August 1963.

We investigated sunken ships on the cruise. Here the author swims down forty feet to inspect the remains of an old ship. Wrecks are always exciting and excellent for pictures. This one is well preserved but many are mere piles of ballast rock, all that has remained of a once proud ship. (Photo courtesy Paul Tzimoulis)

It was a grim little expedition that headed to shore that evening, armed with underwater flashlights and snorkle gear. I honestly believe that those who stayed behind thought they would never see us again. Some said they were going below so they couldn't hear us scream when the deep-sea monsters found us. Actually, it wasn't that dangerous. Mr. Anderson had selected a cove that led to shore where he felt we would be well protected and from there we could take short swims out over the elkhorn reefs with the ultraviolet light. We also had regular underwater lights.

Two girls, Billie Head and Donna Wilt, made the night trip, although I had emphatically stated that this was strictly for men. Women just have to tag along, but no one complained. We made it to shore without incident in the small boat and two trips were needed to haul the group. The water was beautifully clear, very calm, and a half moon lit it up just enough to make the white sandy bottom visible, but not bright enough to destroy the effect of fluorescence from the strange light. It was a weird procession that swam about the dark waters that night, looking like spacemen exploring a new world, which was exactly what we were doing. Actually this was one of the very few times that a portable ultraviolet light had ever been carried underwater on a live coral reef. We swam in ever widening circles, each taking a turn with the weird light. Most corals and sponges would not give off fluorescence, but certain types would fluoresce brilliantly in bright yellows, greens, or deep reds. We saw a fair sized octopus in the shallow water but he gave off no fluorescence. Jerry Smith grabbed him by the head but it squirmed out of his hand. We also saw strange two or three foot long sea cucumbers. They were very sticky to the touch and once one was picked up it was difficult to let it go. After it was

The author with a huge hog snapper and grouper speared in the Bahamas. The hog snapper on the left is one of the most delicious fish in the tropics and a favorite of the skin diver who shoots them for dinner. It is rarely caught by anglers. (Photo courtesy Ralph Bowden)

learned they were harmless, it was sort of a joke to stick them on someone's neck or back as they swam by in the darkness. On tender parts of the skin they caused a definite burn, so eventually the group tired of them and looked for other things.

All of us made "sparks" fly by moving our hands rapidly through the water. Tiny bits of phosphorus would whirl through the water like so many sparkling diamonds and everyone enjoyed the fireworks. We saw a few lobsters crawling about and a fair number of pink cardinal fish and red squirrelfish. Also, a large colony of long-spined sea urchins crawled out on the edge of the narrow channel and several men received punctures from them. One of the best skin divers of the group, Hardy Jones, kept a lookout for sharks by swimming along the outside edge with a powerful underwater spotlight. He would sweep it around in a large circle to watch for any sharks that might move in on us.

The two girls showed considerable bravery by swimming all about without worry. Billie Head took the underwater light and made a long exploratory swim out to the deeper water where it dropped off to twenty feet and more. It was a weird sight to see the dim shadows of men outlined against the hazy glow of the powerful ultraviolet light. The machine made a loud humming noise that added to the unworldy scene. As the time wore on, the men became braver. Some swam out a considerable distance. No sharks were sighted and it was a perfect evening. However, I knew we were pressing our luck for night diving out in the Bahamas is definitely dangerous. I was relieved when the motor launch returned from the ship to pick us up and I am sure Mr. Anderson was also. We returned to the ship with strange stories of what we had seen and no one was eaten by sharks or giant morays. It was an exhilarating experience.

Storms have always been a plague in my skindiving

Interesting coral formations, ancient bottles, and glass floats decorate the author's home. Odd coral formation at left is a nearly perfect duplicate of human arm and shoulder. Small marine aquariums decorate the lower shelf.

career. Fierce tropical storms, which are usually accompanied by high winds and water spouts, are especially frightening to me when I am caught far from shore in a small, open boat. It makes a man feel mighty small and insignificant when the wrath of a huge storm whips the sea into a wild, swirling froth that tosses the boat around like a leaf in a cyclone. I have always been particularly afraid of lightning, and when I am caught out at sea in my boat, I usually drop anchor, put on my mask and flippers, and go over the side. I would rather face the storm in the water where it is warmer and where there is probably less chance of being struck by lightning. I can remember one time that I will never, never forget.

The sun was just setting and since I was many miles from shore I decided to head in while there was still some light. I pulled up the anchor and was about to leave when I noticed that I could no longer see the shoreline. At first I thought it was because of the impending darkness, but then I realized that a gigantic storm had engulfed the entire area, from horizon to horizon. The sea was flat calm and I headed in the general direction of shore at top speed. Suddenly a jagged streak of lightning lit up the darkened sky and the thunderous crash seemed to come from the sea behind me. I slowed down the motor and gazed up. I realized that it would be foolhardy to attempt to reach shore now. My only chance would be to head back out to the reef, anchor, and go overboard until the storm passed.

I soon reached the reef and already the calm sea was rippled by a cool, steady breeze; the forewarning of what was to come. The sky was intense grey and cruel lightning gashed it open in a hundred places at once with ominous clatters of thunder. I never felt so alone in my whole life as I sat in the boat, putting on my flippers and face mask. My bare shoulders were covered with goose bumps, not from the cold, but from the eerie situation I was now facing. Already I could see the fierce storm heading directly for

Huge assortment of collecting gear, glass jugs, enamel buckets, nets, glass-bottomed bucket and heavy outboard motor, which I loaded and unloaded each trip often completely covered with mosquitos. It was a labor of love.

me, and I felt I was doomed as I entered the dark water of the outer reef. The storm came quickly, and soon the seas were whipped into a frothy white mass of foam, so dense that visibility was reduced to mere inches, and I tried desperately to keep the boat in view. I had swam a few hundred feet away, with the thought that lightning might strike the metal motor, and in the turmoil that followed I became twisted around and lost sight of it. Then when I began to search through the monstrous, foamy seas I found that it was gone! I quickly turned around, assuming that it was still close by and was merely hid momentarily by the huge waves but still I could not find it. The sky had now darkened into night and I knew that without the boat I would surely be lost. I began to pray and felt so lonely and helpless and cold as night came on that I began to feel death was imminent and wondered how it would come and what would happen. I knew I would hang on to the last and I knew that with my mask and flippers, I could stay afloat for at least a day, possibly two, but I was in a remote area and already I was drifting north in the Gulf Stream. The chances of even a steamer sighting a nearly submerged skindiver would be slight. Still I began to contemplate what I would do and how I could keep myself alive as long as possible. The rain pelted down like ice-cold bullets and I shivered as it struck me. I began to dive beneath the surface where it was warm, staying under as long as I could hold my breath. Then I would surface and repeat the procedure over and over to keep warm. The sea was now a tumultuous mountain of fury, and as a giant wave lifted me high into the sky, a prolonged flash of lightning illuminated the entire area, so that I could see for miles around. Then, in the far distance, like a derelict in the night, I saw my boat tossing wildly about in the turbulent sea. I thought I was dreaming, it looked so unreal. What am I doing out here, I thought, as I swam frantically in the general direction of the boat. I didn't see the boat again for several minutes until another wave lifted me high into the sky. While I had dreaded the lightning before, I prayed for it now, for without it I would be hopelessly lost.

I swam for a long time at full speed and finally I was within twenty feet of the boat and could see it plainly. It looked so strange to me then. This is unreal, I thought. Why was I able to find the boat now, when I had searched so hard for it before? But there it was, right before me. I paused for several minutes before climbing aboard. I began to think of giant sharks prowling beneath me and wondered if they were just playing with me, like a cat does a mouse. I almost feared to get closer to the boat. Would a shark grab me as I tried to climb aboard, I thought? Then I decided perhaps I was to be spared and I reached for the gunwhales and hung on, half daring the sharks to attack. But none came and I pulled myself aboard.

The boat was partially filled with water and I baled rapidly to keep from capsizing. The storm was abating and I started the motor to keep the boat under control. I gazed fondly at my collecting gear, and my thermos of hot coffee, still stored snugly in the tiny cubicle up in the bow. Everything else was wet but I was thankful to be alive. I pulled in the frayed anchor rope and when the storm finally passed over, the seas calmed and the night was never more beautiful. I drank a hot cup of coffee and headed for Venus, the bright star that marked the way home. It was a night long to be remembered.

Since then I have made many more trips out to the reefs. Skin diving is never dull and although the average trip may be uneventful, it is the unexpected, such as my last encounter with man-of-war jellyfish, which provides adventure. After being almost killed by the jellyfish, I naturally avoided the dreadful creatures like the plague. Last year, however, we had an invasion of them, and the waters were covered with an untold number of the evil things, making diving difficult. While diving I actually scooped up a huge man-of-war that had drifted directly over me.

When I looked into the net and saw the gruesome creature, the whole horrible nightmare of my last attack came
into my mind. I almost got sick. I couldn't believe my
eyes! I had been so careful to avoid the creatures yet one

The author stands in the stern of the small sixteen-foot open boat
in which he explored the seas, usually alone in his quest for aquarium specimens. The bushel basket in the foreground becomes a
floating live well when inserted in the innertube. Collecting buckets contain angelfish, butterfly fish, moray eels, and other specimens for the nation's aquariums. Strong winds on a typical cold
winter day have lashed the sea into a foamy mass which often
leads to adventure or disaster. (Photo courtesy Bob Martin)

came so close to me that I caught it without even seeing it!
It was all I needed to convince me that I shouldn't be out
there that day. I got back in the boat and headed for home.
Skin divers are making fabulous finds in gold and silver

right off our coast. New submarines are coming into use that can let us go deeper and explore new areas. Having had the gold fever once, I will just have to go out to the wreck for another look and perhaps this time, I will find the treasure.

Index

235